Ancient Peoples and Places

REPUBLICAN ROME

General Editor

DR GLYN DANIEL

ABOUT THE AUTHOR

Alex McDonald graduated in Classics from Auckland University College, New Zealand, and Clare College, Cambridge, and studied Roman archaeology in Göttingen, Germany, in 1933; his research covered Rome's expansion in the Mediterranean. He was the first Lecturer in Ancient History at Nottingham, when he undertook to complete the Oxford Text of Livy, thus treating the part that described the period of his historical interests. He became the first Professor of Ancient World History in Sydney University, Australia. In 1952 Dr McDonald returned to Cambridge as Lecturer in Ancient History, becoming Senior Tutor, then Steward, of Clare College; he acted as Professor of Ancient History at Chicago in 1954.

Ancient Peoples and Places

REPUBLICAN ROME

A. H. McDonald

87 PHOTOGRAPHS
11 LINE DRAWINGS
9 MAPS
2 TABLES

London
THAMES AND HUDSON

THIS IS VOLUME FIFTY IN THE SERIES

Ancient Peoples and Places

GENERAL EDITOR: DR GLYN DANIEL

© A. H. MCDONALD 1966
FIRST PUBLISHED 1966
PRINTED IN GREAT BRITAIN BY
WESTERN PRINTING SERVICES LTD, BRISTOL
NOT TO BE IMPORTED FOR SALE INTO THE U.S.A.

CONTENTS

ILLUSTRATIONS

for Martin and Ian

Preface

'WHATEVER you write about Republican Rome,' a candid friend has remarked, 'I'm looking at the pictures first.' Good—I should hate to have the pictures left to the last. But I would prefer to find them also consulted along with the text, for that is how the book was written. What can one add to the standard histories of the Roman Republic? Certainly pictures, using the fresh results of archaeology—not to mention the technique of photographic reproduction; also coin sketches, since historians have neglected to exploit what the numismatists offered them. And maps, not merely to show where things happened but—by visual impression—to suggest how and why they happened: the Romans, like good soldiers, for better or worse, used their eyes in deciding their policy. These features at least, I hope, will make the book worth studying as an illustrative essay.

Modern research has developed our historical interpretation of Rome, in two fields especially which the Romans took for granted: first, the social conditions and sentiments of the ruling nobles; secondly, the character of the Italian peoples who joined Rome and contributed to the Roman citizenship. In the field of economic change, too, where the Romans ignored the factors and complained at suffering the social consequences, we can go further in analysing the Italian situation of the second century BC. The illustrations will help in discussing these matters. We shall treat social history, not forgetting that Republican thought moved in terms of politics, war and administration and was slow to face the responsibilities of conquest.

Rome should not be studied in lofty isolation, as if she had learnt nothing from her neighbours—Etruscans, Italians and Greeks—and then imposed her way of life on passive subjects.

The rise of Rome is much more complex. Therefore I would prescribe reading elsewhere in this series: Raymond Bloch on *The Origins of Rome* and *The Etruscans*, T. G. E. Powell on *The Celts*, A. G. Woodhead on *The Greeks in the West*, R. M. Cook on *The Greeks till Alexander*, J. M. Cook on *The Greeks in Ionia and the East*, and Donald Harden on *The Phoenicians*, which means Carthage. Under Roman power these peoples influenced the growth of Roman civilization, until we have to enlarge—in cultural terms—what we call 'Roman'. The Etruscans did not lose their technical skill with their freedom. In the Late Republic half of Roman Italy was Greek. The Romans belonged to the world they conquered, and in borrowing art forms for their own purpose they were not shopping in a foreign market. We have to bear this in mind in adding Miss J. M. C. Toynbee's *The Art of the Romans* to our list; Sir Mortimer Wheeler in *Roman Art and Architecture* will not let us forget it.

This book is my own—for any merits and in its defects—and I have applied the experience of teaching with visual aids. But the historian depends on expert advice. Anyone who now wishes to illustrate Roman Italy should read Ernest Nash's *Pictorial Dictionary of Ancient Rome* and consult his files in the American Academy in Rome, then ask him to photograph whatever else he wants. In laying stress upon maps as a means of exposition I am not the first to benefit from the skill and advice of H. A. Shelley. I only hope that the reader will relate the maps to my text and pardon the absence of minor places where these would have confused the general effect. It was the late Harold Mattingly who showed me the historical importance of Republican coinage; I am further in debt to R. A. G. Carson of the British Museum, C. M. Kraay of the Ashmolean, and Graham Pollard of the Fitzwilliam Museum. For the coin sketches, where one can feel a quality of art, I am in debt to Elisabeth Amies.

A new feature of this book is the illustration of Republican farming, which throws light on Cato's *De Agri Cultura*. I have to thank P. H. Blanckenhagen and J. B. Ward-Perkins for the (pre-publication) pictures of the Villa Francolise, which is as near as could be desired to the locality of Cato's farm; Mrs Molly Cotton explained the details with kindly care, and I am most grateful to her. G. D. B. Jones has let me use John Bradford's views of Apulian agriculture, and I thank him as well as the Apulia Committee of the Society of Antiquaries; the reader should consult Bradford's *Ancient Landscapes* (1957) about the problems. Then C. E. Östenberg has permitted me to apply his interesting reconstruction of a South Etrurian farmstead—from the magnificent Swedish publication of *Etruscan Culture* (1962)—and I express my appreciation of his scholarly cooperation.

More briefly let me acknowledge help from Richard Nicholls and H. W. Catling, the benefit of discussion with Miss Jocelyn Toynbee, John Ward-Perkins, M. H. Bräude, R. G. G. Coleman, and—on the deep problems of Roman morality—the continuation of many years' talk with R. E. Smith.

The staff of Thames and Hudson have been most helpful about the layout of the illustrations, and—like all writers in this series—I am duly grateful for the support and guidance of Dr and Mrs Glyn Daniel.

The book, which has grown out of my past work, looks ahead in its dedication to my nephews Martin and Ian Dickson and the generation of young historians.

A.H.McD.

HISTORICAL CONSPECTUS

Late sixth cent.
Etruscans	Greek Cumae	Carthage
	Rome under Etruscan kings	
509	Capitoline temple	

c. 500 — ROMAN REPUBLIC

Rome and Latin League: Cassian treaty (493)

Etruscan decline   Oscans in Campania

450   Decemvirate and Twelve Tables

Struggle of patricians and plebs

396   Fall of Veii

390   Gallic sack of Rome

ROME, LATIUM AND ITALY

'Servian' wall (378)   Licinio-Sextian laws (367)

350   Ostian 'castrum'   Rome and Campania

End of Latin League (338)   First Samnite War (343–341)

Roman citizenship, Latin treaties, colonization

Ap. Claudius Censor (312)   Second Samnite War (326–304)

300   Third Samnite War (298–290)

Lex Hortensia (287): patrician-plebeian nobility

War with Pyrrhus (280–275)

Rome's Italian confederation   Silver coinage (*c.* 269)

ROME AND CARTHAGE

'Mamertines' at Messana   Hiero II of Syracuse

250   First Punic War (264–241)

Provinces: Sicily, Sardinia and Corsica

Latin literature: Livius Andronicus and Naevius

Carthaginian Spain: Ebro treaty (226)

Gauls: Telamon (225)   First Illyrian War (229–228)

Hannibal and Saguntum (219)   Second Illyrian War (219)

Second Punic War (218–201)

Cannae (216)   Capua, Tarentum, Syracuse (216–209)

First Macedonian War (214–205)

Loss and recovery of Spain (211–206)

Scipio Africanus: Zama (202)

ROME AND THE MEDITERRANEAN

200 Philip V of Macedon   Antiochus III of Syria

Second Macedonian War (200–196)

War with Aetolia and Syria (192–189)

Third Macedonian War (172–167)

Spanish provinces: Cato (195), Gracchus (180–178)

Cisalpine Gaul: Via Aemilia (187)

160   Social and economic change in Italy

Polybius on Roman imperialism   Cato on agriculture

Hellenistic influence on art   Lex Aebutia in law

Latin literature: Ennius, Plautus, Terence

Rome as a capital city: port of Ostia

150 ## IMPERIALISM AND REVOLUTION

Spanish wars (154–133)   Crisis of recruitment

Third Punic War (149–146)

Fourth Macedonian War (149–147)   Sack of Corinth (146)

Macedonia and Africa as provinces

Roman culture: 'Scipionic Circle', Panaetius, Lucilius

Spain: Numantia (133)   Sicily: slave rising (135–132)

Tiberius Gracchus and land reform (133)

130   Pergamum as province of 'Asia'

Gaius Gracchus, Equestrian Order, Italy (123–121)

Cimbri (113–101)   Marius   Jugurthine War (112–106)

100   Marius and Saturninus (103–101)

The Italian question: Livius Drusus (91)

Social War (91–88)

Roman Italy: citizenship and municipal growth

First Mithridatic War (88–85)   Second Mithridatic War (83–82)

Sulla and the Marians (83–82)   Pompey in Sicily, Africa (82–81)
Sulla's dictatorship (81–79)

80   Historical and legal studies   Hellenism and Roman art
The Sullan 'constitution'

THE LATE REPUBLIC

Optimates and Populares
Aemilius Lepidus (78–77)   Spain: Sertorius (82–72)
Pompey
Spartacus (73–71): Crassus
70   Consulship of Crassus and Pompey
Third Mithridatic War (74–63): Lucullus
Lex Gabinia (67): Pompey against pirates
Lex Manilia (66): Pompey against Mithridates
Pompey's settlement of the East (62)
63   Cicero as consul: Catiline's conspiracy
Caesar governor of Farther Spain (61)
60   Pompey, Crassus and Caesar against Cato and the nobles
The First Triumvirate
Caesar's consulship (59), then command in Gaul (58–50)
Clodius' tribuneship (58)   Cicero in exile (58–57)
Cicero on Italian policy
56   Conference of Luca
Caesar in Gaul, Pompey governing Spain, Crassus in Syria
Crassus' death: Carrhae (53)   Pompey sole consul (52)
Cicero *De Republica*
Civil War (49–45)
44   Caesar's dictatorship for life, and death
Caesarian legislation for Rome, Italy and provinces
Antony, Octavian and Lepidus against the Republicans
The Second Triumvirate (43)
40   Antony commanding in East, Octavian in West
Octavia—Antony—Cleopatra
Actium (31)

18

CHAPTER I

Romans and the Republic

OUR TITLE *Republican Rome* is convenient and roughly descriptive: it marks the period of nearly five centuries from the rule of the kings to the founding of the Empire by Augustus. But it shirks a number of questions; for it represents a collective and constitutional view, in the high Roman fashion, disregarding the stages of growth and changes of character in the Roman citizenship. We do not have to submit to the Roman terms as we study the social and political development.

ROMAN CITIZENSHIP

Who were the Romans of the Republic? The community on the Tiber crossing about 500 BC was already a mixed population, though it had a common Latin culture, enlarged by Etruscan and Greek influence. After destroying the Latin League in 338 BC the Romans took some of the Latin communities into their citizen body and lived in close treaty relations with the others: some of the noblest Romans boasted of their Latin origins. Then, as they increased their power, the Romans extended their system of treaties throughout Italy and organized the social unification of the country, until in 91–88 BC the allies forced their way into Roman citizenship. Rome was now Italy, and Italy became Roman—perhaps even more Roman in respect for the traditions than the sophisticated capital itself. Politically, it is true, the ruling families imposed and upheld a pattern of government; socially the process of expansion was reciprocal, in differing degree at each stage. Ultimately, one may say, it was the clash of obsolete politics with fresh social forces, bedevilled by the use of military strength, that wrecked the Republic, and Augustus' achievement was to take politics out of administration. However, at this point we have only to indicate the complexity of our title: the rest of the book is designed to unravel it.

In Italy as much as in Greece we have to study the effects of regionalism, even though the context involved cooperation rather than rivalry. My maps are designed to illustrate the moves of Roman expansion and the conditions of Italian municipalization under Rome. The various regions retained their local character—Etruscans and Gauls to the north, the Latin centre, the Greeks in the south—and Roman policy respected their diversity, however strongly it applied a general control. The art of Rome—as Virgil said—was not only to conquer but to impose a system of peace. This meant administrative direction, supported by material development, through town-planning and architecture, road-building and engineering, and agricultural settlement. Others might invent: the Romans organized their results. And even when the political storms broke over their heads, they continued this basic work of civilisation, as honest middle-class citizens devoted themselves to the public service; Augustus recognized their value, which allowed him so rapidly to establish the Imperial system.

The Roman historians took too much of the Roman achievement for granted, preoccupied as they were with the moral problems of political power—not that these are unimportant if, as they knew, power tends to corrupt. We have to appreciate how Rome organized Italy but was slow to accept the consequences. Here I return to my illustrations. First, the social tradition that supported policy. Republican art shows this feature, in reference to the noble families and to the ceremonial of the state—but not, in the end, so as to exclude the private claim of Eurysaces the wealthy baker. Next, the rise of Rome in Central Italy, as she freed herself from Etruscan pressure: we can see the desolate remains of Veii. The port of Ostia developed, and by the second century BC Rome had become, in effect, the capital of

Plates 1–18

Plates 19–22

Plates 23–44

Italy—a city, despite the Imperial overlay of building, that is
well worth a Republican visit. But we should not forget her   Plates 45-47
local enemies, who later helped in supporting her greatness.

As Rome incorporated Central Italy and gained experience
in doing so, we may cover the ground in order to view the
older cities and the new foundations like Alba Fucens and   Plates 48-59
Cosa. Here the archaeologists contribute to history. South,
wards then to Campania, with its Greek background, and the   Plates 60-65
Republican remains in Pompeii. The Roman organization and
the investment of spoils of conquest built up the Italian cities,
their markets, and the farming that fed the cities. The Elder
Cato describes how to farm under the new conditions, and in   Plates 66-73
the light of recent archaeological work I am able to illustrate
how this was done. But finally, since the Republic closed in a
blaze of politics, it is necessary, and interesting, to show the
leading historical figures—in sculpture and on coins—from   Plates 74-87
Sulla to Caesar, and Antony, Cleopatra and the young
Octavian; I have limited my choice to contemporary portraits,
along with the relevant coins.

HISTORICAL TRADITION

A national historian, if he interprets an old tradition under
strong contemporary influence, will provide evidence, in effect,
at two levels: first, the basic material for the period he is des,
cribing, more or less documentary according to the degree of
his knowledge; then the attitude of his own period to its past
history, which may be equally significant. Where his material
is scanty, he may elaborate it by pressing its implications as he
sees them, often anachronistically. For example, when and how
was the Roman Republic founded? The story is stylized, in
patriotic and literary terms which cast doubt upon it. The early
relations of Rome with the Latins? Perhaps Rome did not dic,
tate events or the Latins acquiesce as definitely as the later

Roman historians describe. The painful recovery of Rome after the Gallic sack of the city in 390 BC? It may not have proceeded as clearly as we read—unless Camillus was the 'second Romulus'. How far were the party disputes and agrarian prob, lems of the later Republic projected into the earlier period in order to give a pattern to inadequate records? The Sullan age appealed to traditional precedent in a way that might tempt the historians to improve on a fragmentary picture. We have to approach Roman history before the third century BC with caution—and welcome the archaeological evidence that is now coming to light, as well as independent study of the other Italian peoples. Similarly we shall learn something of the later Republic by considering its historical views.

The Romans began to think of themselves historically in the third century BC, after they had repulsed Pyrrhus and driven Carthage out of Sicily. They now ruled the Western Greeks and held a place in the Mediterranean world. But were they still 'barbarians' in Greek eyes? They must prove their honour, able antiquity. Homer had shown Odysseus wandering in the West; even better, an old tradition brought Aeneas, who had escaped from Troy carrying his father Anchises, to Latium, and no Greek need despise a people of Trojan origin. If Aeneas had visited Carthage, and if he had met and parted from Dido, then the clash of Rome and Carthage took on a long perspec, tive. Myth is never far from early history, and the epic poets Naevius and Ennius gave depth to the Romans' view of their past. By the end of the Republic, in more sophisticated fashion, *Fig. 1* Venus and Anchises along with Aeneas would reappear to honour Iulus, Aeneas' son, and the Julian family which had finally produced Caesar and Augustus.

There was also a religious quality in Roman thought. The careful ceremony of public worship, the expiation of unnatural prodigies, the ritualistic apology for war as a breach of the *pax deorum*, for instance, reflect belief in a divine order of nature

a

b

Fig. 1. Aeneas and Anchises
(*a*) *Denarius* (c. *48 BC*). *Head of Venus; Aeneas holding palladium* (*statue of Minerva*) *and carrying Anchises, CAESAR.* (*b*) *Aureus* (c. *42 BC*). *Head of Octavian, III VIR. R.P.C.* (triumvir rei publicae constituendae), *C. CAESAR; Aeneas carrying Anchises, L. REGVLVS IIII VIR. A.P.F.* (quattuorvir auro publico feriundo)

under which gods and men lived in intimate association, and the Roman state must scrupulously preserve its balance. To act like men and appease the gods, according to the ancient rites: this was sound religion and good politics. Surely Rome's success proved the case! And did it not also show that she was fulfilling a divine mission of civilization? Antiochus the Great urged Scipio Africanus to use his victory magnanimously, as Polybius reports, because 'Fortune had given Rome world dominion,' and Scipio replied, 'Victory did not change the Roman policy.' Livy raises the tone: 'Be magnanimous as masters of the world, and lay down your strife with mortals:

like gods tend and spare the human race'; and Scipio is made to reply: 'The gods have granted us what was in their power to grant: our spirit, which is our own, remains the same in every fortune.' The words idealize a traditional attitude.

Roman historiography, however, was more than a patriotic exercise, and we can follow the stages by which it developed, under Greek influence, in terms of material and method. The first difficulty is that before the third century BC there was little direct evidence; the archives were not systematically kept before 300 BC and the previous records may not have gone back in detail more than seventy-five years. The Romans themselves claimed that the Gallic sack of Rome in 390 BC destroyed the earlier records; this may be partly a way of explaining the paucity of information about the fifth century BC. We do not have to dismiss Roman history before the Gallic sack, but we must allow for anachronism in the later attempts to reconstruct it from whatever records survived. From the third century onwards, thanks to Fabius Pictor and the use of his work by Polybius, we are on firmer ground; the historians of the second century had access to the archives and used their family records; and about 123 BC, P. Mucius Scaevola, the learned Pontifex Maximus, arranged for the editing and publication of the priestly archives in the *Annales Maximi*. Since nothing important happened in public life without reference to the priests, we may assume that this collection provided a chronological framework for Roman history under the earlier Republic.

Fig. 2

The first historians were not solemn archivists. Fabius Pictor, who was prominent during the Second Punic War, and his senatorial successors of the second century BC were men of affairs. They discussed the origins of Rome and described Roman policy in their own time, writing in Greek, so as to set Rome in the Mediterranean scene, for the benefit not only of their own cultivated circle but for the Greek public—and all the more so as they felt the need to justify Roman intervention

5th cent. BC	Roman tradition
4th cent.	Etruscan history Greek scholarship Roman records, family stories
3rd cent.	Roman epic Fabius Pictor
2nd cent.	Senatorial historians and Polybius Cato, Calpurnius Piso
c. 123	Publication of archives: *Annales Maximi* Antiquarian study, Greek literary methods, Political bias Gracchan Annalists
1st cent.	Sullan and Late Republican Annalists Contemporary writing: Cicero, Caesar Sallust and Livy Roman biography (cf. Plutarch) Technical: Varro and Vitruvius

Fig. 2. Roman historiography

in the Hellenistic world by reference to her record of policy in
Italy. We are fortunate that Polybius, the Achaean politician
and historian, lived in Rome in the mid-second century,
attached to the Scipionic family, and wrote a comprehensive

history of the imperialist expansion of Rome. He used Roman material as well as Greek, and observed the contemporary Italian scene for himself. Enough of his work survives to allow us to write fully about the conditions of his time, when the archaeological evidence also comes into the picture.

The Elder Cato, whose talent embraced everything that touched the life of Rome, turned the writing of history from Greek into Latin: he inspired the study of antiquarian evidence in Rome and Italy. Under Cato's influence L. Calpurnius Piso, a noble of standing in his own right, and others continued the systematic work of exploiting the archives and providing a learned commentary. It was this development that brought forth the publication of the *Annales Maximi*. At this time, when the Gracchi challenged the authority of the nobles, there appeared two new factors in the writing of history: first, the need to appeal to historical precedent for political purposes, which affected the interpretation of the past; secondly, the influence of Greek rhetoric, which in historical writing stressed the technique of reconstructing a circumstantial account, by pressing the implications of evidence, however scanty it was, in the light of general experience. The Gracchan Annalists made the most of the *Annales Maximi*. Then under Sulla and afterwards, as the tendentious appeal to tradition was intensified, the Annalists elaborated the writing of Roman history, and this is the account that survives in Livy for our use.

Meanwhile historiography had branched out into monographs, *e.g.* Coelius Antipater on the Second Punic War. Sisenna concentrated on the Sullan period; so Sallust could not only write on Catiline and Jugurtha but continue, in his *Histories*, the account of events after Sulla. This was more analytical history, which represented the controversies of the period, and we shall be referring to it later. The speeches and letters of Cicero give us contemporary evidence, as do the *Commentarii* of Caesar. Finally, we have to keep in mind the evidence of Roman biography, as we find it especially in Plutarch, who drew fully from the earlier historical authorities. I would venture to say—and refer to Shakespeare—that the Elizabethans came closer to the Romans through the reading of Plutarch than we do for all our critical rewriting of their history. For the Roman historians, whether like Livy they sup' ported the old regime or like Sallust opposed it, applied the same standards of political morality, and lamented its decline.

Yet social conditions and political factors change, so that the old standards represent obscurantism unless they respect the new conditions, and Rome suffered a major revolution as the penalty of conquest during the second century BC. We shall study this revolution; meanwhile let us search for the wider evidence of social conditions. From the second century BC good Roman antiquarians had worked independently to study the institutions, rites and customs of the state, including the life of the countryside, until at the end of the Republic Varro could combine their results. Archaeology can now help—as my illus' trations show—if we recruit such allies as Vitruvius and broaden our interpretation of the whole historical scene.

The coinage of the Late Republic presents an interesting kind of visual history, sometimes more vivid than reliable, but significant for the political ambitions of the day. The moneyers did not hesitate to glorify their families, just as the earlier his' torians had done. Consider, for instance, the gallery of the Aemilii Lepidi, as they upheld their reputation before the public gaze, until M. Aemilius Lepidus joined the Second Triumvirate after Caesar's death. In the light of our illustra' tions we can write the following account. 'An Aemilius Lepidus serving in the army at the age of fifteen slew an enemy and saved a citizen's life; he was honoured by an equestrian statue on the Capitol, and it is worthy to appear on a coin along with the head of *Roma*.' The most famous of the family in the second century BC, M. Aemilius Lepidus, as a junior

Fig. 3

Fig. 3. Aemilii Lepidi (*a*)–(*c*) *Denarii* (c. *66 BC*); (*d*) *Aureus* (c. *42 BC*)
(*a*) *Head of* (?) *Roma; equestrian statue of M. Aemilius Lepidus bearing trophy,* M. LEPIDVS, AN.XV.PR.HO.C.S. (annorum xv progressus hostem occidit, civem servavit). (*b*) *Head of Alexandria, turreted,* (AL)EXANDREA: *M. Lepidus placing wreath on Ptolemy V,* TVTOR REG. S.C. PONF. MAX. (tutor regis, senatus consulto, pontifex maximus). (*c*) *Head of vestal Aemilia; Basilica Aemilia with shields,* AIMILIA REF.S.C. (Aimilia refecta, senatus consulto), M. LEPIDVS. (*d*) *Head of Lepidus,* M. LEPIDVS III VIR. R.P.C. (triumvir rei publicae constituendae); *vestal Aemilia with simpulum (ladle) and sceptre,* IIII VIR. A.P.F. (quattuorvir auro publico feriundo), L. REGVLVS

envoy delivered the Roman ultimatum to Philip V of Macedon —Philip pardoned his arrogance because he was 'young, hand-some, and a Roman'—and went on to visit Ptolemy V in Egypt; he was consul twice, censor, and Pontifex Maximus;

his organization of Northern Italy left his mark on the Via Aemilia and the Emilian region, and he built the Basilica Aemilia in the Roman Forum. A name to conjure with, especially when Egypt was an object of political interest. 'Let us remind you, as you see the turreted head of Alexandria on this coin, that he was guardian of the young Ptolemy and Pontifex Maximus.' Perhaps he was the young warrior, in the Second Punic War, or it may have been his son. 'An Aemilia was a Vestal Virgin, attending the eternal sacred fire of Rome: the fire went out, but Vesta herself rekindled it for the blest Aemilia; let her head appear on the coin that commemorates how M. Aemilius Lepidus restored the Basilica Aemilia, with its shields' (78 BC); Aemilia may have been the daughter of the Pontifex Maximus. These glimpses of past greatness and divine favour were published by the moneyer M. Lepidus about 66 BC. When M. Livineius Regulus about 42 BC wished to celebrate Lepidus the Triumvir he showed his head and title, along with the figure of Aemilia the Vestal Virgin.

In a similar way, though more directly, the sons of Pompey the Great could display their father's glory on their coins in order to support the cause for which he had died in the Civil War. These are historical instances—in addition to the immediate evidence for the position and influence of public men —where the coins serve our purposes of study.

Plate 81

CHAPTER II

Founding the Republic

SITUATED on the Tiber crossing, it is often said, Rome had the strategic advantage of her position in Italy. The point is less than half valid. An important junction of routes concerns all the neighbours: the people living there are as likely to suffer for their situation as to profit from it. We do not have to be wise after the event, following at the tail of a Roman triumph, as if the city were predestined to exploit its position. In fact, the Romans began by learning the danger, when Etrus/cans took over their site and themselves, and they never forgot the lesson. By their own efforts they turned geography to their advantage; then they went on to extend the topographical prin/ciple until it became a firm strategic factor in their policy.

ITALY ABOUT 500 BC

At the time when the Republic was founded, Rome's situa/tion was barely significant. The field of action was much wider, as three strong powers struggled for predominance in Italy, Sicily and their coastal waters: the Etruscans, the Western Greeks, and Carthage. I show a perspective sketch of the mari/time basin lying between Italy, Sardinia, Sicily and Carthage: it suggests the pressure that could be exercised upon Central Italy, as well as the position by land. Directly across the Adriatic are Epirus and Macedonia, with Greece to the south and the Aegean beyond. The map will serve to illustrate the Carthaginian strategy of encircling Italy in the Second Punic War, while Hannibal held Southern Italy. Then, working outwards, we may appreciate the considerations which Rome applied in the successive stages of her expansion in the Central Mediterranean.

Fig. 4

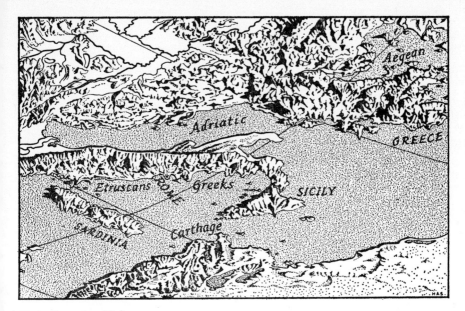

Fig. 4. Perspective of Italy

By the sixth century BC the Etruscan confederacy of cities,
already long established in their own territory, had expanded
northwards into the Po valley and southwards through Latium
—where they held, for instance, Rome and Praeneste—to Campania; and their ships sailed the sea down to the Bay of Naples.
Etruscan commerce made useful contact with the Greeks of
Southern Italy and thus with Greece and the Aegean, as we
know from the tombs of Etruria. Greek cultural influence
accompanied Greek trade, and Rome was amongst the cities
of the Etruscan sphere that drew benefit from it. But the Etruscans pressed too actively, and the Greeks resisted them. At
the same time Etruscan policy, sharp and enterprising though
it appeared, was never coordinated in imperialistic fashion:
individual cities and warlords made their own way, where
opportunity offered; they suffered from internal dissension and
lacked cohesion in external affairs. Towards 500 BC the

31

Etruscans were in retreat from the south, at least by land, after the Greeks of Cumae had checked them in 524 and then lent support to revolt in Latium; these were the circumstances in which Rome expelled the royal Tarquins. In 474 BC Hiero of Syracuse defeated the Etruscans off Cumae, and they lost their command of the sea. Henceforth we have to think of them in Etruria—and in the Po valley until the Celts arrived—that is, concentrating on their own region. Their technical skills, we may assume, were still influential, especially in engineering and road-building, as urban development progressed in Central Italy. This is a point of historical perspective, not to be under-estimated because the Roman historians largely ignored it. When the Etruscans lost their wide power, and even after the Romans reduced them to political subservience, they still played their part in Italian civilization, helped by the scope which the Roman organization allowed to their work.

The history of Greek colonization and urban growth in the West has been well told, and we have only to relate its points of emphasis to the rise of Rome. The cities were carefully sited and comfortably planned—Sybaris the most brilliant example. Hippodamus of Miletus left his mark on city planning, and the rest of Italy would learn in due course. Cities cannot prosper unless they organize their countryside and seek external mar-kets: the Greeks in Southern Italy handled their Italian neigh-bours and kept their connections with the Greek world. They did not lose their political and military energy, especially where in Campania they faced the Etruscans, men of a similar char-acter. By the end of the sixth century BC the Campanian Greeks had consolidated their position against any foreign pressure and were ready to extend their own influence; Rome had good reason, as soon as possible, to open relations with Campania.

Farther south and in Sicily the Greeks had to contend with the Phoenician city of Carthage, which had established its own territory in North Africa and expanded its trading interests in the Western Mediterranean. Carthaginian history speaks for itself, and we shall consider its relation to Rome later. Meanwhile we may note that Carthage's commerce had spread past the west of Sicily, where it held essential maritime bases, on the way to Sardinia and the coastal waters of Italy; if Polybius is right, the Roman Republic at once made a treaty with Carthage. In the south of Spain Carthaginian power controlled the coast and aimed at penetrating inland. The policy was more coordinated and calculating—to make expansion pay dividends—than that of the Etruscans or Greeks. It impinged directly on the Greek interests in Sicily and was limited to Western Sicily after defeat at Himera in 480 BC. But this did not prevent the free movement of Carthaginian ships to Sardinia and the Italian seas, and later Carthage would recover ground in Sicily so as to raise a threat to Southern Italy.

The triple pressure upon the region they occupied taught the Romans what we may call a 'geopolitical' lesson: their position demanded that they should organize themselves so as to use it. Political organization, in all its social complexity, is strengthened by external threat—as the Romans always remembered, when in less happy times they looked back on their early history. The need for common security over-rode their divergent interests within the state. Leading families retained their authority as long as they were competent, and they made concessions in order to hold popular support. The struggle of the patrician and plebeian orders was marked by compromise, until the strongest families on either side allied themselves in a new nobility of office. Thus they could focus their attention upon efficient administration and a sound military system, and establish their principles of diplomacy and war. We shall study these developments in relation to the Italian peoples, once Rome was able to take the initiative. Meanwhile we have to bring the Republic into existence, a task that is more awkward than it sounds; for the Republic was not built in a year.

33

THE FIRST FIFTY YEARS (?)

Tarquinius Superbus, the last of the Roman kings, was a tyrant, and his son Sextus ravished the chaste Lucretia, wife of L. Tarquinius Collatinus; she revealed the crime and 'withal suddenly stabbed herself'. L. Junius Brutus 'acquainted the people with the doer and the manner of the deed':

> The Romans plausibly did give consent
> To Tarquin's everlasting banishment,

and 'the state government changed from kings to consuls'. Thus Shakespeare, and he is no more romantic than the Roman tradition itself. The first consuls were Junius Brutus and Tarquinius Collatinus, the latter yielding place to P. Valerius Publicola, and Brutus and Publicola established the working institutions of the Republic. When Brutus died in battle against the Etruscans he was succeeded first by Sp. Lucretius Tricipitinus and then by M. Horatius Pulvillus, who dedicated the Capitoline temple. The Republic did not lack its group of founding fathers, somewhat artificially assembled!

Now truth may be as strange as fiction, but if we have other reasons to suspect that historical and literary imagination has been active, then we need not be credulous. The Roman account of the founding of the Republic and its early years looks dubious. How could the later writers know the details? Even the Roman tradition had its doubts. Lars Porsenna attacked Rome—Horatius Cocles 'kept the bridge'—and perhaps he occupied the city for a time. Temples of Saturn, Ceres, and Castor and Pollux are dated to the early years of the Republic, though they represent Greek cults which one would expect —in this period—to have entered Rome by way of Etruria. In any event the Romans can hardly have broken their general Etruscan connections, at least in the trade that supported their urban life, even if it declined. The Republic did not isolate itself before embarking upon its imperial destiny. But later

Fig. 5. Capitoline Temple and Brutus

(*a*) *Denarius* (c. *76 BC*). *Head of Jupiter; tetrastyle temple of Jupiter Capitolinus, VOLTEI. M.F.* (*Marci filii*). (*b*) *Denarius* (c. *37 BC*). *Head of Jupiter, CAPITOLINVS; hexastyle temple, PETILLIVS.* (*c*) *Denarius* (c. *60 BC*). *Head of Libertas, LIBERTAS; L. Junius Brutus, first consul, with two lictors and attendant, BRVTVS*

historians could feel wise after the event. Coins show Jupiter and the Capitoline temple, which the Republic inherited from the Tarquins and made the symbol of the state: a six-column style temple, as the ground plan indicates; one coin, shortly after its destruction by fire in 83 BC, shows only four columns (by artist's error), a later coin depicts it correctly. Then we have the head of *Libertas*, and Junius Brutus walking with two lictors and an attendant at the opening of the Republic. We do not have to accept the whole Roman story, patriotic and ideal ized; yet we need not deny immediately that the Romans began to rule themselves about the time they claimed to have done so.

Fig. 5

There is no account to be written here, but a discussion of the matter—a matter of life or death for the infant Republic. We have to decide whether to save or destroy its first half-century. Was the Republic founded about 500 BC or not until, say, 470 or even 450 BC? The comparative evidence is archaeo-logical, incomplete but continually increasing, and we are dealing with a 'working hypothesis', where it is important to define the terms of the problem. The reader will undoubtedly hear more about it.

Italian archaeology takes pride of place; but as regards the present problem we have to turn to Gjerstad, aided by the historical work of Hanell, of the Swedish school of thought. Gjerstad dates the organization of Rome as a city to about 575 BC and argues from the material remains that Etruscan influence increased until, say about 525, Etruscan kings took political control: the two Tarquins, separated by the reign of the Latin Servius Tullius; and this period lasted to about 450 BC, when the Republic was established. Under Etruscan rule Rome imported Greek pottery, which can be dated, *viz.* Attic Black-figure and early Red-figure ware, and such imports con-tinued until about 450. Only under Etruscan rule, Gjerstad argues, was this possible. What then of the first fifty years of the Republic? The Roman historians gave a list of consuls, the chief magistrates of the state, whose names—or most of them—should have been preserved in records if only for purposes of dating. Granted, but Hanell has connected the names with officials of the cult of Jupiter, which admittedly the Etruscan kings introduced: the names could have served for dating, once the Capitoline era opened. Studying the list, Gjerstad finds Etruscan names in the periods 509–490 and 461–448 BC, with none between: the two periods, he assumes, represent the reigns of the Tarquins, the interval that of Servius Tullius; and the Roman historians, misunderstanding the records, turned the last era of the kings into the first era of the Republic. But the

Etruscan names are too few to make a case. Why should some Etruscan citizens not have stayed in Rome after the expulsion of the kings to play their part in the mixed population of the city? What, too, of the developments recorded under the first years of the Republic? The plebeian *concilium* and tribunes, for example. In fact, there is a real problem in the appearance of plebeian names among the consuls before 486 BC, which points to a struggle within the state as well as against foreign enemies under the early Republic.

How do we tackle the problem of this mixed evidence? It is a strict matter of method. On the archaeological side absolute dating is never easy, unless the finds can be externally dated: otherwise, after establishing their relative sequence, one has to *estimate* the lapse of time. Take, for instance, the date for the organization of the city about 575 BC: it might have been about 600 BC, only twenty-five years different, merely the margin of error in an estimate—but this is critical in the present case, for then the regal period could have ended by 500 BC. The Greek pottery confirms Rome's trading connections, presumably through Etruria, after 500 BC. In the light of the archaeological evidence we may believe that Etruscan kings ruled in Rome before 500—for how long? The answer is an estimate. Can we link up with the first organization of the city in the early part of the century? Only by estimating the period of the pre-Etruscan kings. Estimate on estimate, within a century and a half, when we need historical precision!

Here we are changing our ground of evidence—from archaeo-logy, which at least has its own rules, to the Roman tradition, which calls for quite different methods of analysis. The period of the Tarquins, along with Servius Tullius, is more or less definable. But what of the pre-Etruscan kings, shadowy figures, whose chronology—as far as they existed at all—cannot have been known to the later Romans? We simply cannot make an estimate. From 575 BC, and even more so from about 600 BC, the regal period need not have run beyond 500 BC. In any event a case that involves rejecting the early Republic should not use the tradition for the first Roman kings.

So we return to the years 500–450 BC. The archaeological evidence indicates that Rome still had Etruscan connections: the Roman tradition has established the Republic. How far are the accounts consistent? First a general point: political changes do not necessarily destroy commercial relations. The Etruscans were practical traders, familiar with independent cities, while the Romans had to support their urban life. Then we have to allow for the later Roman idealization of Roman history. The historians built up an image of the glorious Republic: we may discount this tradition even on its own terms. But, once we have stripped it of its elaboration, we do not have to deny its basis. Critical history does not knock down ornamental ninepins. Hanell, however, and Gjerstad following him, are more careful in referring the early list of magistrates not to the consuls but to the officials of the Capitoline cult. This is a possible view only if one rejects the Roman tradition. But why reject it, in its basic features? To do so raises as many problems as it removes. We might conveniently begin the Republic about 470 BC, but there is no reason—as yet—to deny a generation of uncertain struggle. The fascination of archaeology is that it always reveals something new, and we may wait for it to do so.

If we do not dismiss the first fifty years of the Roman Republic, we should note briefly what tradition recorded. The Republic was established not necessarily in 509 BC—there was some later adjustment in the calculation of years—but towards 500 BC. The opening events have been subject to historical elaboration. But two annual magistrates, the consuls, took over the executive authority of the king. There were leading families behind them, in particular the patrician families, rural and aristocratic, while plebeian families in the city held their place.

Etruscan warlords like Lars Porsenna may have threatened and even occupied Rome, but they did not destroy the new regime; the Romans, who under Etruscan rule had been able to dominate Latium, agreed to relations of equality with the Latins (the *foedus Cassianum* of 493 BC). Though they were still part of the Etruscan sphere, they fought to break clear politically, and they aided the Latin cities in common defence against the hill tribes. Within the Roman state the plebeian families lost access to higher office but were able to establish their own assembly and its officers, the tribunes of the plebs, in order to protect the rights of the common people, as the nobles protected their dependants. By 450 BC the situation had settled down and no one will doubt that Republican Rome was in existence. From this point we can speak of Roman organization and policy, and consider the Roman methods of expansion and political relationship, which despite setbacks and difficulties would proceed steadily towards the unification of Italy.

CHAPTER III

Italy and Rome

Figs. 6, 7

AN HISTORIAN will visualize the land and its natural conditions, its regions and communications, its frontier areas, with reference to which he has to describe a process of expansion. One may write a survey—a flat, static method, neglecting the part that the eye played from the outset. I prefer to set a physical map and a political map of ancient Italy side by side, and argue about their relationship. If we include the motives of expansion, the argument becomes political as well, and one can trace the broad lines of diplomacy, military moves, and plans of settlement. The Romans thought in terms of topography and control, and this method fits a direct analysis of their policy.

ITALIAN REGIONALISM

At the opening of the Republic, the Romans already knew how their life could be affected by external affairs, through the rivalry of the Etruscans, the Greeks and Carthage, and they were determined to stand their own ground. They were not yet free of immediate Etruscan influence, while Veii lay close at hand up the Tiber valley, and they failed to defeat Veii at Cremera in 477 BC. More important for the future were their relations with the Latin cities which overlooked the plain. Rome was Latin herself, and the city had grown through the aid of Latin and Sabine immigration; her chief families kept social connections with the Latin aristocracy; and there was a tradition of religious connection with the Latin leagues. Rome and the Latins were natural allies, in terms of geography and culture. But where should the leadership be? The Romans had tasted power under the Etruscan kings: their independence now rested upon retaining it. They had a precedent for policy and the stimulus of necessity. We have noted how they entered into relations of equality under the *foedus Cassianum* in 493 BC; then we read of combined defence against the hill tribes of Aequi and Volsci who raided the Latin plain: Shakespeare preserves the tradition of Coriolanus. Rome improved her organization and diplomacy under these conditions: we may note how she extended citizenship, made favourable treaties, and established strategic colonies, developing a policy that would later serve her interests throughout Italy. But we should not underestimate the quality of the Latins, who maintained their religious and political associations in the league of Ferentina until Rome took complete control. It was Romans and Latins who established the Roman power, and we have to think of Latium as the heart of Rome.

Above the lower Tiber on the map we see Southern Etruria, lying between Caere and Veii, where Rome had to set up her northern defences. By 396 BC she had destroyed Veii, and I illustrate the desolate remains. The Etruscan road system Plates 19–22 allowed her to take military measures, while Etruria itself continued its own life. But before this policy could be stabilized, the Gauls of Northern Italy broke through and sacked Rome in 390 BC: the 'day of Allia' kept its black mark in the Roman calendar. Towards 400 BC Celtic tribes had occupied the region of the Po valley and spread southwards down the Adriatic side of the Apennines. They were strongly organized —the Insubres and Cenomani, for instance, the Boii and Senones—and they settled the land around their tribal centres; they also sallied forth in the summer to plunder far and wide. Brennus led a large group against Rome, and the Romans did not withstand their first onslaught. The immediate effect was catastrophic, the later results beneficial; for despite their loss of prestige in Latium the Romans under Camillus set about restoring their position and improving their military technique

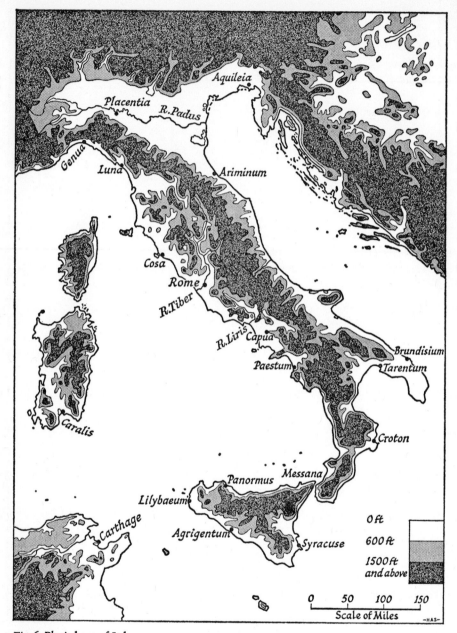

Fig. 6. Physical map of Italy

Area of Roman
citizenship

CISALPINE GAUL

Placentia
Genua
LIGURIA
Via
Bononia
Luna Luca
Via Aemilia
Ariminum
Aquileia
ILLYRIA

Arretium
ETRURIA
R. Tiber
Via Cassia
Via Flaminia
Via Aurelia
Aleria
Cosa
Caere
Rome
LATIUM
Via Valeria
Corfinium
Praeneste
SAMNIUM
Luceria
Via Latina
Via Appia
Cannae
APULIA
Tarracina
Capua
R. Liris
Cumae
Pompeii
Neapolis
Paestum
LUCANIA
Buxentum
Brundisium
Tarentum

CORSICA

SARDINIA
Caralis

Croton
BRUTTIUM

Panormus
Messana
Lilybaeum Drepanum
Rhegium
SICILY
Agrigentum
Syracuse

Utica Carthage

Hadrumetum

0   50   100   150
Scale of Miles
-HAS-

Fig. 7. Political map of Italy before the Social War

Plate 46

in the field. The Gauls continued their incursions until Rome destroyed a large army at Telamon in 225 BC, and they reinforced Hannibal; but in the early second century BC Rome systematically reduced them and organized their whole region. At the same time, since Roman policy now extended to Spain, the hill tribes of the Ligurian area between Pisa and Genoa were pacified so as to secure the land route.

Southwards through Latium and the Liris valley in the fourth century BC the Romans opened relations with the Greeks of Campania, whose chief city was Capua; they saw the profit that could accrue in commerce and culture. But the Samnites lay on their inland flank of communications. An agricultural and warlike people, the most formidable of the prehistoric Oscan-speaking tribes in the central Apennines, the Samnites formed a loose confederation that allowed aggressive military operations, and they had already penetrated into Campania.

Plate 47

Rome determined to remove the Samnite threat. The Samnite wars were hard and ruthless—the Romans never forgot their surrender of an army at the Caudine Forks—and ended with the devastation of the region by fire and sword and the establishment of colonies to control it. The struggle finally drew in Etruscans, Umbrians and Gauls, as a movement of resistance by Central Italy, which failed at Sentinum in 295 BC. Here Rome developed the most brutal of her political methods—to gain security, where cooperation seemed hopeless, by 'making a solitude and calling it peace'. Samnites survived to serve manfully in the Roman armies, but the legacy of ill-will persisted to find outlet in the Social War, when Italy fought to win recognition from Rome.

Once established in Campania Rome extended her influence in Southern Italy, as conflict between the Greek cities and the Italian tribes allowed them to intervene. In this region their frontier kept on moving. By 280 BC Tarentum had called in Pyrrhus of Epirus, the leading Hellenistic general. When

Pyrrhus saw the legions encamped, he remarked, 'The order of these barbarians is not barbarous'; nor was their strategy, for though he beat their armies in the field he could not reduce the strong confederation of Central Italy, with its mountain bas- tions and solid manpower. In the same way Hannibal, for all his control of the south, could not break down the defences of Central Italy. Westwards from the toe of Italy to the ball of *Fig. 4* Sicily the regional association of land and coastal waters brought Rome, like the Greeks before her, into the play of politics against Carthage. Thus we return to our earlier study of the wider spheres of activity affecting Italy. The maps tell nearly half the story—and we shall be able to dispense with further military detail. The rest of the story involves the social and political state of Rome and her relations with the Italian peoples: here we shall find the regions equally relevant to the peaceful development of the country.

ROMAN POLICY

The Romans did not found their Republic or prepare their stages of expansion with the easy superiority of which they boasted later, when they began to idealize their destiny. Yet their progress is marked by qualities of leadership and organiza- tion, both at home and in external relations. They looked hard at things, took firm decisions, and accepted the lessons of suc- cess or failure, in order to apply their experience to the next problem. That is why they would emerge as the greatest lawyers of history.

In public affairs the struggle of patrician nobles and the plebs led more often than not to practical compromise. Thus the plebeian *concilium* and its tribunes rose alongside the full assem- bly of the people, the Comitia Centuriata, which represented the people in military order, while the consuls, with the indepen- dent authority of their *imperium*, and the Senate, exercising its advisory powers, handled the executive side of government. As Rome consolidated her territory, the people could be registered according to locality, under 'tribes', and we meet a new assembly, the *Comitia Tributa Populi*, which would take its place in general legislation. As early as 450 BC private law also took shape. The Twelve Tables under Greek influence codified the old customary practice and brought it up to date in statute form: the citizens could claim their personal rights, and good magistrates would develop it. Only sound administration made such things possible.

Leadership is a personal matter, within its social and political field. If the patrician families took the initiative this was because they had the social standing and personal ambition. Here we have to recall the ancient institution of *clientela*, by which the head of a family as *patronus* accepted the duty of protecting a wider group of dependants, his *clientes*, while they respected their obligations towards him: the bond was extra-legal, one of good faith, *fides*. We need not enter into the complexities of *clientela*, especially in the early period: it is enough to stress that it aided the government of Rome by noble families and gave their members electoral support. Since Roman society remained stable until the second century BC, the institution continued beyond the time when it had a genuine social function; it degenerated into a method of paying for political loyalty, and the great generals of the Late Republic would use it as the basis of appeal to the veteran soldiers they had settled in retirement on the land.

Meanwhile we should note the psychological effect upon the patrons themselves. Exercising moral authority at home, they assumed that they could do so abroad. Thus when the Romans made treaties on liberal terms in Italy, they still took it for granted that their allies would respect their wishes. Often, of course, they were in close social relationship with the allied leaders, and both sides gained by collaboration—it was

Tiberius Gracchus who disturbed these conditions of government in Italy. Another point is relevant to the history of the
early Republic. The patrician families were rural landowners,
while the city of Rome had its plebeian families, no less important in the life of the state. The need for unity against external
threat put a premium on competence in executive office. I do
not think we need trace the course by which the chief plebeian
families gained access to the higher magistracies. We shall only
note that when the Lex Hortensia of 287 BC brought the old
struggle of the patrician and plebeian classes to an end, the result
was to establish a new noble class of leading patrician and
plebeian families, a nobility of office that would be marked by
holding of the consulship, and it followed the old conventions
of aristocratic rule. This class in turn became exclusive, once
the need for unity was over, and the last century of the Republic
shows them appealing to the glory of their ancestors as much as
to their own promise, through history and art—the more
strictly as they met wider political problems, resisting the power
of strong individuals who pressed the claims of talent and ambition to handle the imperial problems of administration throughout the Mediterranean.

Plates 1–6

Fig. 3

ETRURIA AND THE LATINS

We now return to the process of war and diplomacy by which
Rome moved in three stages, first to secure her northern approaches against Etruria, then to organize Latium under her
leadership, and finally—more broadly—to establish an Italian
confederation. Towards 400 BC the Etruscan power was in
decline, already repulsed from the south and under pressure
from the Gauls in the north; but Veii and her neighbouring
allies still disputed the mastery of the Tiber valley. The Romans
pinned Veii down and in 396 destroyed the city and annexed
its territory; then, using the network of Etruscan roads, they

47

Figs. 6, 7

took control of Southern Etruria. They also used diplomacy in negotiating social relations with the well-established city of Caere on the coast. The maps show how these steps served to contain Etruria. The Etruscan cities resumed the life of their region, and we need not underestimate the influence of their industry and commerce. Rome had not enough time to consolidate her defence system before the great Gallic raid of 390 BC broke her army and sacked the city. Later historians magnified the defeat—as if she had failed in her destiny—but the true significance lies in what the Roman soldiers had learnt: they developed tactics to withstand sudden attack and outlast the enemy in the field; then they were able to lend help to other peoples in Central Italy who suffered from the whirlwind Gallic incursions.

Plate 38

The next stage in Latium has wider political implications. The Gallic sack weakened Rome's influence among the Latins, and she set about restoring it by her own efficiency. The city was defended by a strong stone wall—the so-called 'Servian' wall—and Roman troops joined the Latins in repelling the Gauls and the neighbouring hill tribes. There was need to secure social unity, and the Licinio-Sextian laws of 367 BC eased the economic conditions of the people. Civil administration was improved by the appointment of praetors and aediles, officials whose function was to handle the affairs of a growing state. The Latin League gained from Roman help, but the Romans gained more, especially in the south of Latium; a treaty with Carthage in 348 BC shows this. As Rome made contact with Campania, and to some extent with the Samnites on the way, the Latin League felt that its position was being turned and it rose to resist the Roman policy. In 340–338 BC the old friends and allies fought a war: the Romans won the victory and were able to organize Latium under their leadership. The settlement was a practical one. Rome extended her citizenship and imposed treaties that allowed local autonomy—

a system of allied relations which, with due regard for the various conditions, would be applied throughout Italy and even in the provinces. It was an auspicious opening, yet a natural one, since the Latins were familiar neighbours, sharing the Roman way of life and their common interests.

The formula of settlement is clear. Rome became the political centre of Latium without centralizing her rule. Some Latin cities already closely associated with the city, mostly along the southern coast, were absorbed into the Roman state, and two new territorial 'tribes' were established. With the other Latin states Rome made treaties which allowed local autonomy and confirmed the private rights of business dealings (*commercium*) and intermarriage (*conubium*) with her own citizens—though, initially at least, not between the Latins themselves, so as to loosen the ties of the old Latin League. The Latins had to follow Rome in foreign policy, and provide levies of troops for the army, a requirement which at this time involved chiefly common defence; in due course they were able to migrate conveniently to Rome. The Roman relations with Campania led to another category, *viz*. cities with the private rights of Roman citizenship (*civitas sine suffragio*), which was perhaps foreshadowed by the connection with Caere. It was the kind of relationship that Greek cities had with one another for the benefit of their citizens. In any event the cities joining Rome in this way had a Greek tradition, which sustained their civic pride, *e.g.* Cumae and Capua: they were ready to live with Rome, providing they continued their own life, and the Romans respected their wishes. So much for the formula—but we should appreciate the practical background. Rome had taken charge of her Latin kinsmen and hoped to make more of their relationship, as Latium was gradually united; the leading Roman and Latin families knew each other and, once the clash was over, could rely upon mutual support. These were early days of economic development, so local affairs could be left to the individual cities; yet, if there were an external threat, as from the Gauls, they would all need to combine under strong military leadership. The settlement was flexible in normal times, efficient in an emergency. With the Campanian cities the relationship was satisfactory on both sides.

In this context we have to note the policy of colonization, by which settlements were started at strategic points in order to secure the neighbouring regions. The Latins had established the system, and the Romans with Latin help developed it. The policy had to be adapted to the local conditions. At some points, especially on the coast, it would be difficult to create a sound community: the garrison aspect would predominate, small allotments of land would suffice, and the settlers would continue to look to Rome; here the colonists retained full Roman citizenship. At other points a settlement, for all its primary purpose, might enter into the regional life and grow as an urban community: the colonists would benefit from larger allotments of land and develop municipal institutions; here the colonies received Latin status, and Roman citizens were glad to join them. Their function was not to cow their neighbours, as the Roman citizen colonies had to defend the coast, but to influence local life and, in case of need, provide a secure base for the Roman armies. I shall not list all the colonies or show them on the map, but only stress that inland colonies, which had to make their own life as well as provide potential bases, were mainly Latin colonies, and they contributed to the unifica, tion of Italy. The conquest of Samnium enlarged their scope, first strategically, then as a means of Romanization.

Fig. 17
Plates 50, 51,
54, 55

ITALIAN CONFEDERATION

Close relations between regions and key points of control with, in a country call for good communications—that is, roads—and the Romans had learnt this principle from the Etruscans. My

map shows the roads radiating from Rome to coordinate the *Fig. 7*
life of Central Italy: the Via Appia to Campania, the Via
Flaminia northwards, and the eastern routes across the Sabine
hills. Along these roads armies and merchants could put the
miles behind them.

Close relations also demand better administration at the
centre. As the focus of Latin life, extending her interests to
Campania, Rome had to improve her routine methods of
government and organize the city as a capital. That is why
Appius Claudius Caecus, the censor of 312 BC, attempted to
raise the political standing of the urban citizens. He failed in
his immediate purpose, against the opposition of the rural
nobility; but he set Rome on her new course. His monuments
are significant—an aqueduct to increase the water supply of the
growing city, and the Via Appia to facilitate communication
with Campania. It was his secretary Cn. Flavius who published the forms of legal procedure and a list of court days, so
that the people had ready access to justice. The archives were
now more systematically kept, if it is no coincidence that the
historical tradition henceforth appears in regular order. At the
same time the Samnite wars forced the army to enlarge its
organization of supplies and apply wider principles of strategy.
Beyond Campania and Samnium the diplomatic relations
with the Greek cities and Italian tribes would be more formally
handled. We have reached the stage of professionalism in
Roman administration, both civil and military. Rome had
learnt her lesson liberally in Latium, ruthlessly in Samnium,
and now she shaped it into a policy that could be impersonally
carried out, with the strength to support it. When the new
patrician-plebeian nobility emerged in 287 BC, the leaders were
able to enforce their will, and the patron's assumption of moral
authority was reinforced by technical experience.

When the Etruscans joined the Samnites in an attempt to
reassert their position, Rome defeated them and forced their

cities into alliance, on reasonable terms which made them part of her defences against the Gauls. The Samnite confederation was broken up into its tribes, so that they could no longer act together, and Latin colonies were settled at key points. Pyrrhus and his allies saw the strength of the Roman organization of Central Italy, and when Pyrrhus withdrew the Greeks and Italians of the south felt the impact of Roman policy upon their future. Rome extended her system of treaty relations. It left the cities and tribes free to handle their local affairs, under such obligations of service as might be required. The system, we may hold, involved two kind of treaties, 'equal' and 'unequal', the former stating simply the rights and obligations, the latter including a clause that explicitly recognized the hegemony of Rome. There must have been variations according to the situation and importance, the previous political attitude, and the degree of reliability of the local leaders, and in dealing with these distant peoples Rome could not take acceptance of her authority for granted. But the main principle was clear: Rome would allow local freedom in time of peace but insist on support if there were any emergency involving the whole country under her leadership.

Looking at what we may call the Italian confederation, its members bound by treaty ties to Rome, we have to appreciate how well its organization fitted the social and economic conditions of Italy at that time. I have tried to illustrate Italian regionalism. By now, under the stress of events, Rome and Latium and the nearer Etruscan cities and Campania were closely linked together, and their intimate association overrode the formal distinctions in an area of common interests. Farther afield, and especially in the south, the local life predominated, and for the moment it was best to leave it alone. But suppose economic development brought closer association here too, and conditions in one place affected those of its neighbours? Brigands on the main routes, for instance, if the local authori ties could not cope with them? Rome would need to coordinate law and order, despite the rights of local autonomy under the treaties. We shall discuss this problem when it arises in the second century BC and meet its consequences in the Social War. Meanwhile we must turn to the immediate effect of Rome's conquest of Italy—her clash with Carthage in the Central and Western Mediterranean.

Chapter IV

Roman Expansion

THE CLASH of Rome and Carthage has raised broad historical questions ever since Polybius described the Roman conquest of the Mediterranean. *Vae victis*—and the Romans damned the memory of the Phoenician city they had feared desperately under Hannibal and then brutally destroyed. Why did the two powers open a life-and-death struggle? The two civilizations, it is said, were incompatible: Carthage with her fiery Phoenician religion and culture, Rome with her firm Latin tradition. Yet they had kept treaty relations for over two centuries. Polybius dates their first treaty to the beginning of the Republic, and there was certainly a treaty in 348 BC. We may attribute the initiative at that time to Carthage's commercial policy, while Rome was acquiescent. Rome and Carthage could co-exist, providing they kept their distance. Geography and the map—we have to study the Roman advance in Italy and the Carthaginian position in Sicily.

CARTHAGE AND THE WEST

The Sicilian historian Philinus recorded an agreement in 306 BC defining the Roman and Carthaginian spheres of influence: Rome in Italy, Carthage in Sicily. Philinus was pro-Carthaginian, while Rome had reason to forget any such pact, so we have to admit our doubt; but if Rome spoke for Italy, she would hardly have forgotten the Western Greeks in Sicily. Rome and Carthage consulted about Pyrrhus in 279 BC, as both had good cause to do, and this may have implied recognition of their respective spheres; but the Romans stood only upon what was explicitly laid down. Their relations were probably equivocal. When they clashed, we have to look for the

Fig. 8. Map of Central Mediterranean

practical considerations. Carthage was ruled by a commercial oligarchy, who made war to support their trade: they had monopolized the Western Mediterranean from Spain to Sicily, and from Sicily they pressed their enterprise into the basin lying between Sardinia and the Italian coast; their bases in Sicily were essential, and they used their army to keep the Sicilian Greeks penned in the eastern part. Once Rome conquered Southern Italy, her interests followed those of the Greeks before her, as Pyrrhus had shown strategically: she would react against Carthaginian activity in eastern Sicily, and her experience in Italy would dispose her to take preventive measures, as opportunity offered.

Fig. 8

55

We need not enter into details. The position in Sicily turned upon the resistance of Campanian mercenaries in Messana, the 'Mamertines', against Hiero of Syracuse; the Mamertines appealed for support first to Carthage, then to Rome. Both powers responded, and the clash of policy brought on the First Punic War (264–241 BC). Let us pass over the course of operations by land in Sicily, until Panormus and Lilybaeum brought the Romans to a halt, and Regulus' attack on Africa proved abortive. The Romans embarked upon a naval policy, using their South Italian allies: naval success always depends upon shore organization. Rome won the war by sea around Sicily and then expelled Carthage from Sardinia—here it was a bare matter of military power, regardless of political claims. Thus Sicily became a Roman province, followed by Sardinia and Corsica. How far could Rome apply her Italian principles to Sicily, even modified as they were in Southern Italy among the Greeks? Sicily had to be governed by a praetor, but within the island it was possible to grant special rights. The rule of Syracuse could be recognized, and some Sicilian cities had earned the privilege of treaty relations. For the rest Rome imposed taxation, along the lines laid down by Syracuse (the *lex Hieronica*), in order to cover the expenses of administration. This was reasonable 'occupation policy', and it would be developed in the further expansion of Rome.

Meanwhile we have to consider the effect upon Carthage. The merchant oligarchy cut its losses in the Central Mediterranean and turned to the further exploitation of Spain, not only by trading methods but through more direct control inland; the tribes would resist, and Massilia, the old Greek city and ally of Rome in Southern Gaul, might feel her interests threatened in north-eastern Spain. Militarism followed commerce, as Hamilcar Barca, the hero of resistance in Sicily, took charge in Spain: he hated Rome and feared her strategic drive, alert to maintain Carthaginian power. Where he subdued the Spanish tribes, he recruited their warriors into his armies, and Hasdrubal and Hannibal followed his policy, against the day of war with Rome. Massilia did not let Rome ignore the Barcid aims. In 231 BC the Romans queried Hamilcar's intentions in Spain, but made no move except to open relations with Saguntum, which already had Massiliote connections. In 226 BC they agreed with Hasdrubal that the river Ebro should divide their spheres of influence—but Saguntum lay south of the Ebro. In 219 BC, when Rome appeared to encourage an anti-Cartha-ginian party in Saguntum, Hannibal captured the city—so as to anticipate another Messana—and the Romans counted this a case for war. The Second Punic War lasted from 218 until 201 BC, and Hannibal transferred the focus of operations from Spain to Italy.

In brilliant battles from Cisalpine Gaul past Lake Trasi-mene to Cannae, Hannibal shattered the Roman armies. The capture of Capua and Tarentum gave him control of Southern Italy, in communication with Carthage. Yet, like Pyrrhus, he could not break the strategic strength of the Roman organiza-tion of Central Italy, which Fabius Cunctator used in solid defence. Carthage then enlarged her strategy by operations in Sicily, where Syracuse came over, and in alliance with Philip V of Macedon; the map (compare my perspective map) shows *Fig. 4* the plan—picking up the old policy against the Etruscans and Western Greeks. Rome fought back in all fields until she had recovered Capua, Tarentum and Syracuse, and negotiated peace with Macedon. Time was on her side, and time also raised up the man in Scipio Africanus. His father and uncle had died campaigning against the Carthaginian armies in Spain, and he succeeded to their command. After capturing Carthago Nova he defeated the Carthaginians at Baecula and Ilipa, and returned to Italy to face Hannibal; reinforcements for Hannibal under his brother Hasdrubal had been intercepted on the Metaurus river. Scipio transferred the war to Africa, forced the return of Hannibal, and finally defeated him at Zama. The peace settlement disarmed Carthage, leaving her autonomous but confined to her home territory, as a client state of Rome, while alongside her Masinissa of Numidia built up his kingdom.

How brief and bald—yet the summary gives an impression! Rome waged war in deadly earnest and Hannibal fought to kill, without any play of political compromise. The Romans lost men, allies and territory almost to the point of no recovery: they recovered through their political firmness and the organiza/ tion of their manpower, until Scipio Africanus could devise victory. Their triumph did not obliterate the memories of fear and danger. Hannibal completed their military education and, after their own fashion, they absorbed the lessons into their political thought. We have to allow for the influence of pure militarism upon Roman policy during the following period of Mediterranean expansion.

THE ROMAN WEST

In 201 BC Scipio Africanus celebrated a Roman triumph over Carthage on the Capitol, where he made due sacrifice and handed his laurel wreath to Jupiter Capitolinus. The god and his people faced a formidable aftermath of the long war: they increased their difficulties, in ways that were then unpredictable, by extending their victories throughout the Mediterranean. Within sixty years Rome won an empire and, in so doing, changed the character of her society. Other nations have experi/ enced the same development, with its call for political readjust/ ment, but few made it ultimately so hard for themselves. The ruling class were too rigid and powerful in their tradition, and the arts by which they had gained success were inadequate to maintain it in peace. The course of policy is worth serious study and illustration.

In Italy, as they recovered ground from Hannibal, the Romans had punished disloyalty, especially at Capua and Tarentum, and tightened their control over Southern Italy; in Sicily they had annexed Syracuse and adapted the organization of the province to the new situation. But they did not depart from their basic policy and aimed only at restoring the earlier political conditions of regional life. The process was not so simple. Peasant farming may return to normal once the men come home. Farming that serves urban markets must wait on the rehabilitation of the cities, and the southern cities had suf- fered severely under Hannibal's occupation and their liberation by Rome, such being the nature of military liberation. There had been a considerable shift of population—quite apart from measures like the enslavement of 30,000 Tarentines by Rome— and the drifting elements might well move into the cities. Nearer Rome, of course, the demand for labour in the war industries attracted men from the country, Latins for instance to Rome itself; and the Etruscan cities expanded their production of arms to support Rome's widening operations. Thus urban life in Italy grew more intense, under conditions that were partly favourable, partly disturbing, and this would lead to social unsettlement. By providing fresh markets the develop- ment would affect the scope and methods of agriculture, at least for those who could take advantage of it, the men with money and slaves. But we have to wait for the capital invest- ment that followed the spoils of further conquest. For the moment in Italy the Romans were content to regain political control, while they took up the uncompleted tasks remaining from the war.

The immediate need was to organize the West, where Rome now superseded Carthage in Spain, and this also involved measures to secure the communications by land, especially against the Cisalpine Gauls and Ligurians of Northern Italy. We have already noted the Celtic settlement which established

Fig. 9

the 'Cisalpine Gaul' of Roman history; the Ligurians, a prehistoric people, still held out under harsh conditions, a danger
to their neighbours, in the north-western Apennines. The
Cisalpine Gauls, who had reinforced Hannibal, still maintained their warlike independence within striking distance of
Etruria. From their mountain villages the Ligurians could raid
the coastal strip that lay between Pisa and Genoa. In ten
years the Romans subdued the great tribes of Boii, Cenomani
and Insubres in Cisalpine Gaul, and strengthened Placentia,
their colony on the Po; then they built the Via Aemilia and
set large Roman colonies on the road in order to control the
region. It took longer to reduce the Ligurians to order, just as
it is hard to win a guerrilla war, but by 180 BC the western
route was safe. The map shows the significance of these operations: better still, take a trip from Genoa down to Pisa and
across to Bologna!

All Spain was divided into three parts: the north-east with
Saguntum, where Massilia exercised influence; the south from
Carthago Nova to Gades, where Carthage had held power;
the centre and north-west, occupied by the free tribes of Celtiberia and Lusitania; and the Celtiberians threatened the eastern
region of Spain. Scipio had extended Rome's relations with
cities and tribes during his successful campaign, but his personal authority was short. Roman forces remained in Spain,
and in 197 BC Rome organized her jurisdiction in two provinces, Hispania Citerior in the north, Hispania Ulterior in
the south. There was little effective control, however, until Cato
as consul in 195 BC took charge, and he made no impression
upon Celtiberia. In the settled regions of the north-east and
south Rome followed the policy she had established in Sicily,
by recognizing the local rights of cities (like Saguntum and
Gades) and friendly communities, though her system of taxation was unwelcome. It was not until Sempronius Gracchus
in 180–178 BC, by arms and diplomacy, had established firm

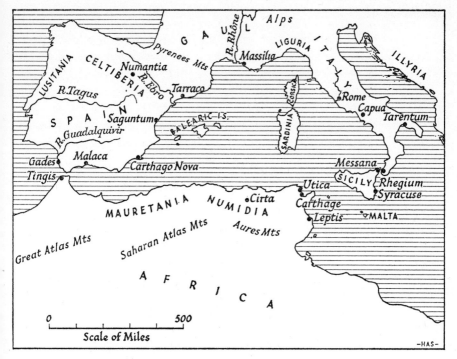

Fig. 9. Map of Western Mediterranean

relations with the Celtiberian chiefs that the Spanish provinces were reduced to order—and that only for a generation; for the tribes were quick to resist anything that smacked of exploitation.

In the West, had she been content simply to replace Carthage, Rome might have enlarged her traditional policy into an imperial system without injuring her own way of life. But she also intervened in the East, too soon and too successfully for her own social and political good. Suppose Rome had drawn the whole of the West together and thus carried on her political development, the process would have been slow but sound, and her entry into the Hellenistic world later would have found Italy less vulnerable to the economic and social consequences.

Pure speculation! True, but we know the catastrophic results of Rome's actual policy: how the further war effort in the East and its quick profits in new wealth for both state and individuals, even where this assisted urban growth and its supporting agriculture, speeded up the emerging process of economic change to a point at which social behaviour lagged behind, among the ruling class as well as the people; and how the material benefits that accrued to the exercise of political power tended to corrupt the standards of public morality.

THE HELLENISTIC WORLD

No sooner had Scipio Africanus triumphed over Carthage than Rome turned her eyes to Greece and the Aegean. Let us recall the general background there before we consider her policy. The conquests of Alexander the Great had brought Greek settlement in their train, as young men moved to the growing cities of the Middle East, which offered a Hellenized life under municipal conditions and scope for administration or commercial enterprise. The whole region, with its varied resources and industries and its old trade relations, lay open to further development through the common use of Greek methods, and governments as well as individuals were systematic in promoting their economic interests. Wherever Greeks lived, for all the differences of locality and native custom, they enjoyed the conventional features of Hellenistic civilization, and their culture now made an easier appeal to other peoples than it had done in the Classical days of the city-state. Rome, of course, was no stranger to Greek influence; she knew the Greeks of Southern Italy, and since her defeat of Pyrrhus she had been in contact with the Hellenistic world not only in the Aegean but in Egypt. Educated Romans traced not only Trojan Aeneas but Greek Odysseus to the West, and Latin writers had taken up the theme; more Roman nobles than

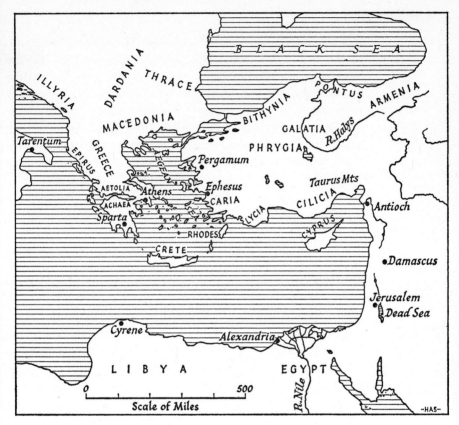

Fig. 10. Map of Eastern Mediterranean

Fabius Pictor understood the Greek language. But these were select contacts, not affecting the Italian mood of Roman life. It was a different thing, especially in her condition of social change, for Rome to enter into popular relationship with Hellenistic civilization.

We have also to regard the situation from the Greek point of view, since the Hellenistic states would ultimately succumb to Roman power. The opportunities which Alexander had bequeathed they sacrificed by political rivalry. His empire was

Fig. 10

split into three major kingdoms: Antigonid Macedon dominat‐ ing Greece and the Aegean, Seleucid Syria with Asia Minor, Mesopotamia and the eastern region extending to the Indus, and Ptolemaic Egypt ruling the Nile valley from Alexandria, the great powers of the Hellenistic world. In the play of politics some smaller but important states would have their part: the kingdom of Pergamum defending her Ionian neighbours against the Celts of Galatia, the republic of Rhodes devoted to the freedom of the seas, and in Greece the Achaean and Aetolian Leagues, the first supporting Macedon, the second bitterly resisting her. The balance of power was only just stable, for geography had created points of strategic dispute. As be‐ tween Syria and Egypt, who should control the Lebanon passes and the sea around Cyprus? Whoever did so would have an advantage, so they made war in order to avoid defeat. From Alexandria the Ptolemies aimed at exerting maritime influence in the Aegean, where they clashed with Macedon. In Western Asia Minor and Thrace Seleucid policy claimed ancestral rights, against the Macedonian interests. A triangular contest of debilitating power politics, and we have evidence to show how Hellenistic prosperity rose and fell with the waging of war. History shows only one other example of such fratricidal folly—in modern Europe! The penalty was to provoke the intervention of Rome and suffer her heavy hand.

Such was the situation when Philip V ruled Macedon and Antiochus the Great had strengthened Syria, two able and ambitious kings, and the young Ptolemy V (Epiphanes) suc‐ ceeded to the throne of a weakened Egypt. Macedon and Syria had less at stake in their rivalry in Ionia, for in the past they had both lost ground to Egypt. Thus in 201 BC, when a report spread that Philip and Antiochus were in alliance to divide the Ptolemaic possessions, it found credence in Greece; Poly‐ bius, using Achaean sources, records a pact. Attalus of Per‐ gamum, an ally of Rome, and the independent Rhodians, who were already fighting Philip, also believed it, and they appealed to Rome to restore the balance. The Romans had not forgotten how Philip joined Hannibal to wage the First Macedonian War at their expense. If Philip with Hannibal could threaten Italy, might he not do so again with Antiochus, who was formidable by land and sea? Then prevent the possibility: limit Philip to Macedonia, check Antiochus in Asia Minor, and guarantee the freedom of Greece as a neutral area! The conception was strategic, following the lines of established Roman policy: one need only refer to my perspective map. The diplomatic procedure applied both the Roman method of recognizing the local rights of friendly states and the Greek principle of autonomy, which Philip was violating by aggression in the Aegean. But were Philip and Antiochus so closely allied as the report suggested? More probably they had merely agreed to leave each other a free hand in enforcing their respective claims against the Ptolemaic empire, a move in the play of Hellenistic power politics. If so, then Roman militarism made too much of the situation and Rome blundered into her course of Eastern conquest, with its portentous consequences for herself and the Greeks. One need not attribute the Roman expansion to a grand imperialistic design, however inevitable it appeared to later historians; yet there was something dynamic about the way in which, often by trial and error, one step led to another, and Rome was too strong to be checked. 'Latent imperialism' it has been called, but our definition must be more than a label. We shall follow the process in Greece for the thirty-five years during which Rome defeated both Philip and Antiochus, tightened her hold on Greece, and then destroyed the Macedonian kingdom.

Fig. 4

In the Second Macedonian War (200–196 BC) Rome formed a coalition of Greek states against Philip V, among them as her strongest ally the Aetolian League, which resumed the alliance of the First Macedonian War. Flamininus defeated

Philip at Cynoscephalae and proclaimed 'the freedom of Greece'; his peace settlement limited Macedonian power and confirmed the autonomous rights of the Greeks, even against one another; and the legions withdrew. The Aetolians resented Rome's assumption of superiority and complained bitterly that the settlement ignored their merits and sacrificed their interests. Meanwhile Antiochus, who had not hastened to Philip's help, moved westwards to reassert the old Syrian claims in Ionia and Thrace. Rome met him with a demand that he respect the rights of Greek autonomy in these parts and not cross into Europe; he replied, reasonably, that this was not Rome's business. In fact, we may conclude, she was determined to extend the neutrality of Greece to the Aegean and Western Asia Minor as a single strategic region. The Aetolians saw a chance of recovering their initiative: they offered to join Antiochus and brought him over the Aegean. In the Syrian War (192–189 BC) Rome crushed Aetolia, expelled Antiochus from Greece, and—with Scipio Africanus in the field—defeated the king and Hannibal again at Magnesia. The peace settlement removed Syrian power from Asia Minor and reduced the Aetolian League to the status of a subject ally; Manlius Vulso subjugated the Celts of Galatia, then the legions again withdrew, leaving Greece to her local politics, while Pergamum grew in importance.

Fig. 11

The Greeks continued their rivalries, now intensified by social conflict, and they did not hesitate to appeal to Rome against one another. Envoys travelled back and forth across the Adriatic as local disputes multiplied, and the Senate hardened its attitude. In these circumstances, when Perseus of Macedon regained some influence and Eumenes of Pergamum appealed to Rome, the legions returned once more to Greece. The Third Macedonian War (172–167 BC) destroyed Macedon; Macedonia was divided into four republics, and Epirus was enslaved. Rome also took steps to subvert the power of

Fig. 11. Macedonian Wars

(a) Denarius (c. 105–104 BC; L. Marcius Philippus). Head of Macedonian king (? Philip V), wearing skin helmet with goat's horns, MA, φ (Philippus). (b) Greek gold stater. Head of Flamininus (on reverse T. QVINCTI, perhaps issued by Flamininus himself). (c) Denarius (c. 55 BC), reverse. Trophy, on left Perseus of Macedon and his two sons, on right L. Aemilius Paullus, TER (Spain, Liguria, Macedon), PAVLLVS

Pergamum and weaken the prosperity of Rhodes. At the same time, when Antiochus Epiphanes of Syria invaded Egypt, her envoy forced him to retire. Where was Greek freedom now? Rome had disrupted the Hellenistic system that supported Aegean life, and left only economic distress and domestic strife in its place; she had stretched her arm into the Eastern Mediterranean.

ROMAN IMPERIALISM

Let us consider the growth of Roman imperialism. We have to envisage a process developing in three phases, the first two in conjunction leading to the third. First, Rome's strategic policy represented a mixture of suspicion, calculation and preventive action, which did not cease working even in the hour of success; for every advance raised further problems. This was the dynamic militarism of Rome, backed by political initiative and professional skill. Rome sent the legions beyond her frontiers to forestall possible danger and, when they returned, she held them in readiness to move again. Next—the second phase—wherever Rome entered, she might withdraw her power but she left her influence, indirect but serious. When she guaranteed the rights of her friends and allies, Rome did so first as leader and then as patron, tacitly expecting that they would respect her wishes 'in good faith', above all in matters affecting common security. Freedom whether in Italy or Greece should not be abused through the pursuit of discordant aims: in Italy Rome enforced arbitration between her allies, so why should she not offer firm advice to the Greeks? The Greek states did not appreciate such unwritten obligations nor did Rome clarify them—if, indeed, it was possible to define her assumption of discretionary control; in Italy the allies had learnt compliance. The Greeks were more resistant: Flamininus had declared them free, so why should they not exercise their rights at home and in their local relations, friendly or hostile? Moreover, where they had old claims against their neighbours, why should these lapse? At least they should be able freely to settle their own disputes. Against this view Rome could argue that the principle of autonomy now precluded aggressive action among the Greeks themselves, and her envoys were capable of applying the case to local conditions. Perhaps Roman patronage and Greek politics were incompatible: in any event neither side attempted to understand the other. Only Scipio Africanus was capable of handling Hellenistic affairs liberally and, when he attempted to influence the peace settlement with Antiochus, he was driven out of Roman politics.

The Aetolian warmongering brought Roman militarism and diplomatic methods closer together in common practice, ominously, to open a third phase. When Rome reduced the Aetolian League to formal subjection, this was a strategic measure to secure her approach from Italy to Central Greece. Elsewhere, on the Aegean side, she kept to the use of senatorial envoys, but they acted more brusquely and less scrupulously. Resenting this arbitrary and harsh treatment the Greeks still aimed at circumventing it, or even exploiting it in local rivalries, through cleverness. It was a dangerous legalistic game, which Rome could play equally well, and ultimately she was umpire as well as player. Even more dangerous was her habit of turning a series of improvizations into a convention, which her representatives would follow as a new set of rules. Thus patronage became openly dictatorial and diplomacy took on features of political terrorism, partly in direct action, partly by exploiting civil strife within the Greek states. Individual Romans made matters worse—Q. Marcius Philippus, for instance, by sharp practice and such men as C. Popillius Laenas by brutal arrogance. In fifteen years the Greeks suffered the consequences, when Rome intervened once more against Macedon: in 167 BC no one escaped the penalty of the Roman peace.

The Third Macedonian War had brought a fresh factor into this phase of policy, *viz.* a crisis of military confidence. As the campaign dragged on, the Greeks—even perhaps Pergamum—hoped to negotiate peace, and Rhodes proposed mediation. Rome sent out L. Aemilius Paullus, followed by a second army in Illyria, and won the war; but the circumstances increased the part of militarism in the mixture of her diplomatic methods. That is why she destroyed the Macedonian kingdom, subverted the power of Pergamum, and reduced Rhodes to helplessness. If Epirus needed control as the Adriatic bridge-head into Greece, why otherwise enslave its Molossian population? It was the honourable Aemilius Paullus who carried out this policy. In the Greek states Rome supported factions which persecuted Macedonian supporters, and accepted a thousand hostages from Achaea—including Polybius. Greece was still nominally free, but even local freedom was, in effect, drastically limited. And Popillius Laenas would draw a circle in the Egyptian sand round the king of Syria and demand an answer to the Roman ultimatum before he stepped out of it. These were systematic measures, and they became a precedent for policy, infecting Roman conduct in every sphere. We can now speak of imperialism in its initial stage of repression, as it applied power without sense of responsibility to the subject peoples. Twenty years later Mummius would sack Corinth and Scipio Aemilianus, as honourable a man as his father Aemilius Paullus, would weep over Carthage only after he had obeyed his orders to destroy her utterly.

Power, we know, tends to corrupt—but there were also social factors at work in Rome and Italy during this period, and we have to turn to the condition of Rome herself.

CHAPTER V

Rome and Italy

HANNIBAL had failed to destroy Roman power, and final victory left the Senate and its ruling nobles firmly in command; but he had disturbed conditions in Italy to an extent which called not only for rehabilitation but for social readjustment. The consequences, exaggerated by the Eastern wars, were such as to affect the basis of Rome's military system and her conduct of domestic affairs in Italy. We have first to consider the economic situation.

In Southern Italy, where Hannibal's occupation and the Roman reconquest had inflicted the most direct suffering, the problem in fact was simplest. After the disruption of regional life, it was left to local enterprise to restore normal conditions. Here the cities and large estates, once they had resumed their old relations, could lead the way, while no war prevents peas/ants from returning to their land; the displaced part of the population had their chance of settling down in new urban or rural life, however difficult the process might be. When Rome let out her public land again, it was taken up by local landowners, who farmed it in the confidence that they would have security of tenure. Seventy years later their descendants might be shocked when the Gracchan policy of close land settlement terminated their leases, but meanwhile it aided recovery.

ECONOMIC CHANGE

In Central Italy the situation was socially more difficult. Rome's military levies had spread the young men on service, while the growth of war industries to supply the armies brought others into the cities, and many restless veterans might join their number. Rome itself was the centre of attraction, though the Etruscan cities were busy and Campania made a rapid recovery. Overseas campaigning continued to support this economic development. We should consider the result. A larger urban population means a larger market for agricultural produce. Rome, for instance, had to undertake more building operations; the trades required leather and wool; the workers and their families, not to forget those who catered for them, needed grain and meat, oil and wine, which had to come cheaply and conveniently. The city imported grain in bulk by sea from Sicily, and this expanded the port of Ostia and its shipping; similarly Eastern trade used the Campanian port of Puteoli. The other food supplies had to be provided locally, if agriculture could adapt itself to the market demands. Production of this kind was not the work of peasant farming but of specialized agriculture with resources of capital and cheap labour which would enable it to establish olive groves and vineyards and develop the pastoral side. The methods were familiar in Etruria and Southern Italy, and they were encouraged by the urban growth of Latium and Campania. The influx of wealth and slave labour from Mediterranean conquest had yet to take economic effect, but we can already discern the pattern of development.

It is worth while studying the closer relations of Rome and Latium. In 193 BC Roman money-lenders were found to be using Latin agents in order to avoid the restriction of Roman interest rates, and Rome brought these transactions under Roman law. A fair measure—but did it violate Latin rights? In fact, the commercial life of Latium had moved beyond the conditions envisaged in the treaties. At the same time Latins were migrating to Rome, where they could get work and acquire Roman citizenship by residence, and the Latin states had difficulty in supplying their quota of troops; in 193 BC the consul accepted only a proportion of the men liable for service. But would this be enough to keep the Roman armies up to strength? In 187 BC, as the drift continued, Rome agreed with the Latin authorities to repatriate Latins who had migrated since 204. Another violation of Latin rights, even though by agreement! In fact, the social life of Latium had rendered the system of Latin levies obsolete; but the army still took precedence. Why did the Latin authorities support the illtreatment of their people? Presumably because, as local gentry, they felt no interest in those who left their city, but were concerned to keep the relations with Rome that bolstered their own position. The point is significant, if the Italian confederation now worked through the personal alliance of the Roman and allied leaders. Yet social change is not so easily checked. As Rome flourished, the Latins resumed migration. An arrangement by which they should leave a son at home proved ineffective, and by 173 BC the Senate had again repatriated recent Latin immigrants. This was no way to maintain stable social conditions. The trend was probably general, though less intense elsewhere. Campania grew closer to Rome, and cities there with private rights of citizenship received the full rights, while the ancient Greek city of Cumae adopted Latin as its official language.

By 187 BC the long period of major warfare was over, and Rome could enjoy the profits of conquest. The treasury, which had been empty at the close of the Second Punic War, was now replenished by indemnities and the spoils of war from the wealthy East, and showed a surplus. The Senate repaid the citizens $25\frac{1}{2}$ imposts of war taxation, and we learn of an abundance of money on the Roman market in 186 BC. Let us glance briefly at the Roman coinage. Over eighty years earlier, about 269 BC, Rome had issued her first regular coinage, in silver didrachms and associated bronze, modelled on the Greek coinage of Southern Italy. It was planned not for use in Latium but to assist her new relations with the Greek cities of the south after the defeat of Pyrrhus. It served its purpose during the First Punic War; then, modified in a second issue, it continued to the eve of the Second Punic War. At this point Rome made a new issue, based on the *quadrigatus*—a didrachm with its associated bronze—in an attempt to unify her coinage; it was still directed towards the Greek cities, especially for the share they would take in preparations against Carthage. Hannibal's occupation of the south cut short this issue, it would seem, and when Rome was able to counter-attack southwards she made another issue, the coinage of the silver *denarius* with its associated bronze, by 211 BC—at least this is what fresh evidence from Sicily now suggests, rather than a later dating to 187 or 169 BC. In due course the growth of Rome as a capital city must have brought the *denarius* into circulation there, by as early as 186 BC. The coinage was suited to Italian commerce and to Mediterranean relations, as Rome expanded her power; and so it would remain, after a change in its standard in the late second century BC.

We have also to note the influx of Eastern money into Rome at this time, at least part of which must have passed into currency. The record of the booty carried in triumph will serve as illustration. In addition to works of art and unwrought silver and gold, Flamininus brought back 84,000 Attic tetradrachms and 14,514 'Philippi' (gold staters). The Scipionic triumph over Antiochus is worth listing:

> 224 military standards, 134 models of towns, 1231 ivory tusks, 234 golden crowns, 137,420 pounds of silver, 224,000 Attic tetradrachms, 321,070 *cistophori* (tetradrachms), 140,000 'Philippi' (gold staters), 1423 pounds of chased silver vases, 123 pounds of gold vases.

The metal, wrought or unwrought, and part of the coinage might be melted down for bullion, but 'Philippi' and Attic and cistophoric tetradrachms could pass into currency in Italy.

There is little scope for statistical argument about Roman economics, but one example is interesting. The repayment of the war tax was made out of Manlius Vulso's booty from Asia

Minor in 187 BC: if all the booty were used, the property value on which the tax was levied, during the Second Punic War, may be estimated, as a maximum, at 1000 million *denarii* (say £40 million sterling on gold standard). It may, of course, have been less, but property values must have risen in the first half of the second century BC. An estimate of the sum of indemni- ties and booty recorded for this period gives, as a minimum, 250 million *denarii* (£10 million). In 157 BC the treasury had coinage and bullion valued at only 25 million *denarii*; since we have omitted the normal revenue of the state, we may assume that the profits of conquest had all been used on military expendi- ture or public projects. The figures suggest the degree of finan- cial stimulus to urban life and industry where we have noted the new pattern of economic development: it must have been revolutionary in its social effect.

The Roman censors not only held the census of the people and kept the roll of the Senate and *equites*: under the Senate they also let out the contracts for public work; and the early second century BC is marked by influential censors, who applied Rome's resources to her material development. The public contractors, drawn from the class of *equites*, increased their wealth and economic significance, while their craftsmen and labourers benefited with them. Polybius appreciated their importance. In all the areas of Italy under Roman administra- tion, he says, innumerable contracts were let out for the construc- tion and repair of buildings and for the collection of revenue from the use of rivers, harbours, gardens, mines and land; some people took up the contracts along with their partners, while others backed their undertakings with the state.

Thus far on the subject of state policy; the field of private investment does not allow any estimate, but it must have ex- panded enormously. Generals and officers brought back their personal spoils from the East, according to the rules of Roman warfare, and they put their money into land, the legitimate type of business for the senatorial class and the security that cannot fly away. The effect was to speed up the progress of adapting agriculture to the needs of the urban markets, especially in Latium and Campania. Here we have the evidence of Cato's *De Agri Cultura*, in which he offers advice to senatorial investors: though he praises life on the land, his aim is to show them how to make a profit. For the average estate he recommends the production of grapes, vegetables and olives rather than grain: a vineyard of 60 acres with 16 slaves, an olive grove of 160 acres with 13 slaves and free contract labour at the height of the season, along with grazing on leased public land. He has in mind the urban markets which required wine and oil, vegetables and meat, leather and wool. We shall return to Cato in describing rural life later, with reference to my illustrations; for the moment it is enough to show the economic significance of his book.

Finance then—but what of labour? The new farming in Central Italy could make use of slaves, while the great estates of Etruria, Southern Italy and Sicily always needed fresh supplies of them. The reconquest of Southern Italy and the wars of expansion had reaped their regular harvest of slaves, but the numbers coming to Italy were probably not excessive. Now, at the moment when the influx of wealth had boosted investment in land, there was an enormous intake of slaves. In 176 BC, after Sempronius Gracchus crushed a revolt by Sardinia, he boasted—and Livy quotes the inscription—that he had killed or captured 80,000 of the inhabitants: probably the larger part of this number were sold on the Roman slave market, 'nothing cheaper', as the saying went. In 167 BC the enslavement of 150,000 Epirotes must have caused a glut. Later Roman writers associated the growth of large estates and slave labour with the social degeneration of Italy: the free peasantry disappeared and rural conditions were brutalized, especially where the size of estates allowed gang methods of slavery; the slave wars in Sicily during the later second century BC illustrate the consequences.

We have attempted to set the development in economic perspective, but our final impression may well approach that of the Roman writers. As we have noted, the enslavement of Epirus marks a policy that went beyond the strategic case for safeguarding Rome's entrance into Greece: it suggests a mood not entirely due to the difficulties in Greece. Let us now ask another question. Did mass slavery appear at the full tide of rural investment purely by coincidence of foreign and domestic affairs? The answer may show the Senate in a worse light. If agriculture could now increase its profits by using cheaper labour, labour that was plentiful enough to be partly expendable, then use warfare to expand the slave trade as opportunity offered, in rebellious areas like Sardinia and Epirus. Here is imperialism in a stage of exploitation. What of the disregard for the free men of Italy? We must keep abreast of the economic changes, for rural labour was probably already unsettled and ill adapted for work on the larger estates. At the same time it was a drastic step to flood the countryside with slaves who must be kept under brutal conditions. The effects of conquest may have been unpredictable to the Romans: their own social traditions, to which they appealed in other things, should have prevented them from exaggerating these effects. We shall let later events speak, and turn to the character of the Roman leaders and their attitude towards Italy.

ARISTOCRATIC RULE

Though Scipio Africanus gave a keener edge it was the steel of Rome's military power, wielded by the nobles, that brought victory over Carthage. We may recall how they had raised their prestige during the third century BC and proved their ability in the First Punic War; yet they still had to reckon with the mood of the people. Popular support made Flaminius consul in 217 BC—to die at Lake Trasimene; it put Terentius Varro in command for the dark day of Cannae. Thereafter Fabius Cunctator restored the nobles' control of government, and they extended it in preparation for Scipio's final success. Nor could Scipio's military glory override their political influence. Popular feeling sent him against Antiochus when Hannibal appeared at the king's side; but once he tried to impose his views of liberal policy, the nobles charged him with malpractice in the East and drove him out of politics. Hannibal's legacy, in short, was to confirm their regime. It was aided by the strong Italian traditionalism that Cato represented in words and action. We have to open our study of Roman government in the second century BC by recognizing the predominance of the nobles.

Let us move among the Roman nobility, as they receive their friends and clients, against the background of ancestral distinction which it was their duty to maintain. Their attitude was aristocratic: that is, they thought in family terms of a public career and honourable reputation, and brought up their children in the same belief. Able sons had first call, and a family without sons would adopt boys from their more fortunate political allies, while their daughters found a career, through marriage, in cementing political relations. 'I have arranged a marriage for Cornelia,' said Scipio Africanus to his wife, according to the story. 'But surely, Publius,' she said, 'you might have consulted me about my daughter, even if the man were Sempronius Gracchus.' 'It *is* Sempronius Gracchus,' he replied. There was heavy family pressure on the boys to shine in legal work and military service as a preparation for public office. 'Why do you ignore me, Polybius?' said the young Scipio Aemilianus, son of Aemilius Paullus adopted by the Scipios. 'Everyone thinks I lack Roman character because I don't like the law'. And when Polybius reassured him, 'Thank you,' he said, 'I shall feel worthy of my family and my ances' tors.' And this was the man who would destroy Carthage and crush the Spanish tribes at Numantia!

We have Scipionic epitaphs that confirm the impression: 'Cornelius Lucius Scipio Barbatus, son of Gnaeus, a brave and wise man, whose form matched his virtue, who was con' sul (298 BC), censor, aedile among you: he captured Taurasia, Cisauna in Samnium, he subdued all the Lucanian land and took hostages.' Or, 'My conduct increased my family's virtues, I had children, I rivalled my father's deeds: my honours have ennobled my stock.' And if a man died young, 'His life, not his honour, fell short in honours, unsurpassed in virtue: he died at twenty.' Virtue is that of political achievement, the honours those of office. A noble's son was dedicated to a public career, and Scipio Aemilianus betrays the family pressure that could be exerted upon him. For the code was laid down, demanding conformity, and it had only to be fulfilled. Of course, there was rivalry for success in gaining the chief offices of state, but— after Scipio Africanus fell in 187 BC—this turned less on politi' cal ideas than on personal ambition and family influence, with' in the common terms of aristocratic policy. One may speak of the rule of 'the ten families', or at most twenty. Yet the con' vention suited the period. If a crisis arose, able men would emerge momentarily to sway affairs—men like Aemilius Paul' lus or Scipio Aemilianus; yet it is significant how faithfully they complied with the tenor of senatorial opinion. We are able to use the technique of 'prosopography' to study individual careers in their relationship with family groupings: the results are instructive for the functioning of government, so long as we do not treat the groups as parties of a different political colour.

While Roman society kept its traditional character, what was good for the great families was probably good for Rome. The consequences of expansion, especially in the East, brought a change at home not only in material conditions but in personal

Plate 4

attitude, and then the old ideas proved too rigid, even among the best men. As for the weaker members of the nobility, if they abused the power of office, the Senate knew how to discipline them: the censors revised its roll strictly, and Cato's list of prosecutions shows how keenly he watched the state of public morality. It can be no coincidence that in 181–180 BC we find the first law against electoral bribery and the Lex Villia Annalis regulating the steps of an official career. The real danger was more subtle, more implicit in the changing values of Roman society. Juno Moneta of the mint, like Langland's Lady Mede in a similar period, would charm a new generation away from its ancestral standards, and the path of office might lead not to honour but to selfish pride and profit. An aristocratic code assumes tacitly the privilege of practising it, whether or not it be responsibly fulfilled, so that even liberal policy should stop short of destroying its basis; the corollary is to deny opportunity to fresh talent.

These are general terms, falling easily into Sallust's Roman style, because the problem is a general one. We have to insist that it was a process through which social forces eroded the aristocratic morality for a half-century. A special factor was the exploitation of clientship. The noble families relied not only on their public reputation but on the personal support of citizens, many of them migrants to Rome, who respected the old dependence on their patronage, and they used their wealth to reinforce the sentimental ties. We do not yet have to think of a venal proletariat that could be bribed into electoral assistance, for the people were prosperous enough; but the conditions lay open to political corruption.

It is important not to oversimplify the social relations now emerging in Rome. The urban population was mixed, variegated, and volatile. Workers from Central Italy and the south, free men and slaves, had come in. Soldiers returning from the East, who had campaigned under conditions that encouraged licence, brought back their bad habits. But we should keep the general instability of rapid urbanization in mind, as the balance shifted from the countryside. The nobles represented a combination of soldiers, lawyers and landed gentry—like the Prussians—even when they lived in the city and farmed with money and slaves. In 186 BC the Senate believed that the worship of Dionysus, the Bacchic cult with its orgiastic rites, had become a threat to public order; it set up a severe enquiry and regulated the cult. By contrast in 179 BC a reform of the Comitia Centuriata, the assembly of the Roman people for state business, aimed at increasing the voting power of the city bourgeoisie in order to gain steady support for the Senate. The measures were inadequate, if one may judge from the atmosphere of the Third Macedonian War. The war proved tedious and difficult: generals oppressed their Greek allies, soldiers sank into slackness and insubordination; popular agitation increased at home. When Rome called on her best general, Aemilius Paullus, to take command, he had to impose discipline at home and in the field before he won the war. However, victory restored the unstable balance, and Polybius could describe Rome about 150 BC with a mixture of hope and foreboding in his interpretation.

SENATORIAL GOVERNMENT

Aristocratic authority was exercised in Rome through the consuls and Senate, with allied tribunes standing by. The long period of warfare, in which the experienced Senate acted as a war council, had strengthened its administrative position. Constitutionally an advisory body, the Senate had assumed the main functions of direct control—in policy, appointments and finance—and used its legal skill to secure its prerogatives. The consuls served the Senate because their families already formed the magic circle within the body, while the plebeian nobility provided tribunes; the popular assemblies lacked initiative of their own.

Polybius came to Rome after the Third Macedonian War, a distinguished Achaean leader and already a practised historian. Moving in Scipionic circles he felt the dynamic power of Roman imperialism, and he embarked on the history of Roman expansion from 220 BC to his own time in a *Universal History* of forty books; his work is a lamp of Republican history at its critical point. In particular, as he studied Rome's recovery after her defeat at Cannae, he used his experience to describe the administration of the state as he saw it. Like most Greeks Polybius thought in constitutional terms of the growth and decline of systems of government, as power tended to corrupt rulers. From primitive kingship to regular monarchy, then lapsing into tyranny, the process led to aristocratic rule, which narrowed into oligarchy; the people enforced democracy, only to slip into mob-rule, out of which tyranny re-emerged to begin a fresh cycle. Greek history suggested the formula. How far was the cycle inevitable? Perhaps it was a biological phenomenon. Or could one control the process by mixing monarchy, aristocracy and democracy, so that each element might check the corruption of the others? As for Rome, Polybius knew consuls like Aemilius Paullus, the successors to the kings: they were the executive heads of state and supreme in the field. He saw the pervading influence of the aristocratic Senate, dominant in diplomacy and finance. And he recognized the legislative importance of the popular assemblies. Each element of government, he concluded, had powers which counterbalanced those of the others. Why then do we stress the leadership of the nobles? Because Polybius' practical observation was better than his theory, and he enables us to adjust the context.

Rome—to apply modern terms—had 'representative' but not 'responsible' government—like the constitution of the United States of America, which borrowed Roman ideas, and not like British parliamentary practice. That is, on the executive side the consuls were elected but, once elected, they exercised their own *imperium* of office, limited only by law, as the American President does. Lift the legal restrictions by emergency decree, as the Senate assumed the right to do, and the consuls were the masters of Rome, for the period of the emergency. The Senate always enjoyed the prerogative, let us say, of 'advice and consent', to which it now added a certain scope of initiative. The assemblies of the people, meeting in their centuries or tribes or in the Concilium Plebis, were the legislative congresses, normally deciding questions that were proposed to them by their presiding officials after consultation with the Senate, that is, by the consuls or tribunes, as the case might be. Thus the nobles, as they applied their personal influence, could indirectly impose their will on the state. Then politically, though not constitutionally, Rome was at the stage of aristocracy declining under social pressure into oligarchy? Perhaps Polybius after all did have the formula! For tribunes could act independently, as Polybius admitted, and powerful tribunes like the Gracchi could go directly to the people; or, if the tribunes lacked power, a consul like Marius could do the same. Hence democracy in practice, and when it lapsed into mob-rule, there was the dictatorship of Sulla to succeed it. Indeed, the cycle would roughly repeat itself after Sulla, until Augustus established the Empire.

Turning to Italy, Polybius has an instructive passage. Crimes in Italy requiring public enquiry (he states) such as treason, conspiracy, poisoning or brigandage, as well as arbitration between the allies, were handled by the Senate. What of the treaties that recognized local autonomy? Here was the rub. For the social and economic development of Italy since the Second Punic War had brought the regions together. Treason and conspiracy in one place could now spread to others; the virus of an epidemic did not respect boundaries, and it gave rise to suspicions of poisoning; more travel made brigandage a matter of common concern. In a word, Italy was ripe for an extension of Roman citizenship. But the Roman and Italian leaders hesitated to take the step, so long as they could contrive measures of public security. There had to be a legal case, and we find it by returning to the repression of the Bacchic cult. The worship of Dionysus was widely spread in Italy, from Etruria to the south. How then could one regulate it locally? Only by declaring a 'state of emergency' that would justify Rome in issuing instructions to her allies; so the Bacchic question took on a political definition as the 'Bacchanalian conspiracy', an illegal association to subvert the Italian confederation. The danger was surely exaggerated: the point lies in the procedure which the Senate followed in Rome and throughout Italy—to proclaim an emergency, give the consuls powers of martial law, and pass detailed orders to the allies.

Fig. 12

An inscription publishes the consuls' letter communicating the Senate's decree. It closes like this: 'That you proclaim these [regulations] during not less than three market days and, so that you might be cognizant of the Senate's vote, the vote was as follows: if there were any who acted contrary to what is written above, they resolved that the charge should be made a capital one against them; and that you should inscribe this on a bronze tablet, so the Senate resolved [to be] proper; and that you order it to be affixed where it can be most easily read; and that those Bacchic [places], such as exist, except there is something sacred there, as is written above, in ten days after this letter is delivered to you, see to it that they be dispersed'; added, 'In Teuranian territory [in Bruttium].' The translation is literal, no more clumsy than the local scribe's résumé of the consuls' conclusion. The Senate had decreed what should be the form of publication, even under allied jurisdiction, and the consuls passed on the instructions as a report, not omitting the penalty.

We can see how the Senate controlled their Italian allies, and the general implication of the procedure is significant.

```
        HAICE · VTEI · IN · COVENTIONID · EXDEICATIS · NE·MINVS · TRINVM
NOVNDINVM · SENATVOSQVE · SENTENTIAM · VTEI · SCIENTES · ESETIS · EORVM·
SENTENTIA · ITA · FVIT · SEI · QVES · ESENT · QVEI · ARVORSVM · EAD · FECISENT · QVAM · SVPRAD
SCRIPTVM · EST · EEIS · REM · CAPVTALEM · FACIENDAM · CENSVERE · ATQVE · VTEI
HOCE · IN · TABOLAM ·     AHENAM · INCEIDERETIS · ITA · SENATVS · AIQVOM · CENSVIT
VTEIQVE · EAM · FIGIER · IOVBEATIS · VBEI · FACILVMED · GNOSCIER · POTISIT ·   ATQVE
VTEI · EA · BACANALIA · SEI · QVA · SVNT · EXSTRAD · QVAM · SEI · QVID · IBEI · SACRI · EST
ITA · VTEI · SVPRAD · SCRIPTVM · EST · IN · DIEBVS X · QVIBVS · VOBEIS · TABELAI · DATAI
ERVNT · FACIATIS · VTEI · DISMOTA · SIENT     IN AGRO · TEVRANO
```

Fig. 12. 'Bacchanalian Decree': Consuls' letter (186 BC)

There is no more formidable weapon in the hands of any government than the power to intensify police action by arbitrary reinterpretation of the law. This is how dictatorships make a first parade of legality. Sixty years later the Senate would turn this weapon to domestic politics, against the supporters of Gaius Gracchus, and establish it by precedent for subsequent use. We have here the germ of the 'ultimate decree' for defence of the state, which brought legalized force into party politics. For the moment it was an expedient to overcome the difficulties of an obsolescent political system in Italy.

ARMY AND PEOPLE

While in peace the consuls (as Polybius describes) controlled administration and summoned the people together, in war they handled the preparations and conducted the campaigning—by virtue of their *imperium*—with almost absolute power; they supervised the call-up of legionaries and imposed the levies on the allies, according to the treaties. In other words, Rome treated civil and military government as one function, and Roman citizens and Latin allies lived a martial life. This was

85

traditional: the Comitia Centuriata, which carried formal legis-lation, represented the people in army organization. We are more concerned to study the situation in the second century BC, when social conditions were changing. During the Second Punic War most Romans and Latins of military age and fitness who were qualified to serve must have learnt military discipline, and this undoubtedly increased civilian morale. The wars of expan-sion took many men into the Roman army, so that it was still an institution of Central Italian life. But overseas and colonial warfare has not the direct appeal of patriotic defence—the Roman people at first rejected war against Philip V of Macedon —and no military organization continues for long much better than its methods of recruitment. Long-term liability, even though with short-term service, based on conscription: this needs more stable conditions than those following the Second Punic War in Italy; we have seen how Latin migration embar-rassed the Latin states with regard to their military levies.

A Roman qualified for military service in terms of property, as the obligation of a citizen to the state, and he was liable to be called up between the years of seventeen and forty-six, as neces-sity required: a militia system, adapted to home defence; but there was nothing old-fashioned about his training. Hannibal had taught Rome what professional war meant; the overseas campaigns improved her organization of operations, communi-cations and supplies. The Roman, then, did his service, under severe conditions in the West, more profitably in the East—but to what did he return? Changing conditions lowered the pro-perty qualification as well, perhaps, as the quality of conscripts. On the other hand professional warfare had its attraction as a career, especially for men who could rise to centurion's rank, and the consuls could draw upon experienced volunteers in any levy. No doubt the Latin authorities had the same difficulties and the same kind of assistance; for their contingents became, in effect, integrated with the legions.

Army life—as Polybius describes it by the textbook—was well organized and strictly controlled from staff level to the ranks. The levy itself was a measure of public discipline carried out systematically. Staff officers were specially chosen, often men of great experience, and they chose the troops and administered the military oath. The Latin states providing contingents followed the same procedure by their own authority, except that their staff officers were Roman in order to coordinate tactical operations. The staff officers chose their non-commissioned officers, in particular the centurions, and the senior centurions had initiative in the field. That was how the flexible legions defeated the rigid Macedonian phalanx, once it no longer used strong cavalry as its offensive arm. Such tactical initiative depended upon thorough training, and the same applied to the allied wings. Every army, moreover, went out fully equipped from personal arms to siege engines, from the supply system to medical services. The general routine on campaign was laid down by army regulations. The camps were constructed to a set plan, whether permanent or marching camps; guard duties and visiting rounds were fixed; and discipline was severe. At the same time pay and provisions were regular, and decorations were properly awarded; there were rights of plunder and the donatives of generals in triumph. This was good professional organization for maintaining armies in the field, even under undistinguished generalship; its excellence lay in the staff officers and centurions. Sound training and successful campaigning had their educative value in Roman life for the men who served under such conditions, not least for the allied troops now experiencing Roman methods.

Yet no military system can rise far above the state of its manpower—its readiness to serve, the conditions of warfare, its prospects after demobilization. We have noted the developments in Italy, affecting both recruitment and resettlement. Overseas service introduced new factors: in the West it was too severe, in the East too lax; and it involved return to an unstable social situation. The Third Macedonian War revealed the difficulties in the civilian attitude at home, the morale of the army in Greece, and the dissatisfaction even after victory. Aemilius Paullus experienced it, while Polybius would live to see it worse.

Let us return to the Roman camp and take up a larger question. It is for this reason that I have illustrated Polybius' textbook account rather than sketch the remains of a contemporary camp (*e.g.* at Renieblas near Numantia in Spain). We have to treat his camp as half of a balanced four-legion camp (that is, under both consuls), the two parts set back to back on the headquarters side. The normal army comprised only two legions—with allied wings—and its headquarters lay across the *via principalis* so as to be covered by the legions; but the military practice is the same. Within the ditch and rampart, which had its gates symmetrically fixed, the ambulatory way ('intervallum') allowed easy communication and concentration in defence; the internal chessboard pattern of streets and system of blocks were convenient and familiar. The camp could be measured and set up, its accommodation arranged, and its defence organized against emergency, all by a strict routine for which the troops were trained. How did the Romans develop this technical feature? The military writer Frontinus thought they copied Pyrrhus, a master of the Greek method; yet Pyrrhus himself, we may recall, noted the order of their camp. In any event—and here the question opens out—we find a regular plan about seventy years earlier in the 'castrum' of Ostia which was built for defence at the Tiber mouth: it quartered the area by crossroads leading to four symmetrical gates. Even if it had a ritual origin—for instance, in marking the regions from which to practise augury—the arrangement had military value for stationing heavy-armed infantry, whether in legionary camps or in fortified towns; we find the Ostian 'castrum' plan in

Fig. 13

Plate 24

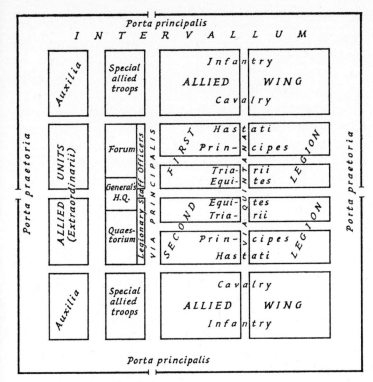

Fig. 13. Roman Camp (Polybius)

towns from the third century BC onwards. This is not the Polybian chessboard plan of encampment, and the Romans might
have learned its details from Pyrrhus. But not necessarily so;
for the Etruscans had apparently used it already at Marzabotto
near Bologna. Certainly we find it at Cosa, a Roman colony
in Etruria, in 273 BC, so soon after the Pyrrhic War that we
should probably allow a longer development. The Samnite
Wars had put system into Rome's military administration, and
this must have affected the routine of the armies.

CHAPTER VI

Roman Culture

URING THE OBSEQUIES of a notable Roman in the second century BC his body was brought into the Forum and set upon the Rostra in full view of the people: his clients would make the crowd. Men wearing the masks of his ancestors sat by him, dressed according to rank, upon ivory chairs. A son or near relative delivered a funeral oration on his virtues and public achievements, recalling the family's glory which he had upheld. After his burial the family added a wax mask of him to the gallery of ancestral portraits, each enclosed in its wooden shrine. Thus the Roman nobility, past and present, gathered to honour and display their tradition and, in their home, to place it on record; we owe part of our historical information to their archives. The custom—as Polybius describes it—was an old patrician one, which was taken up by the plebeian noble houses and continued to serve the piety, pride and ambition of the Late Republic. The wax masks were not necessarily death masks, for Hellenistic influence helped Roman art in keeping its portraits alive. By the end of the Republic masks had given place to busts (wax, terracotta or stone), but Plate 1   the personal impression was the same. I show the late Augustan statue of a patrician carrying his ancestors' busts (in a funeral procession): in different first-century BC styles they presumably represent the original heads.

TRADITION AND ART

From the third to the second century BC the nobles' patronage and control had dominated the course of Roman culture. I have already quoted Scipionic epitaphs (p. 79), which record the performance—or the promise—of civic virtue, and in particular

that of L. Scipio Barbatus, consul in 298 BC. We can also see
his sarcophagus of local stone from the 'Tomb of the Scipios'. **Plate 4**
It has Ionic volutes on its lid and a frieze of triglyphs and me-
topes (each with a rosette), Greek enough in detail but Roman
as a whole; we find a similar pattern in the Sullan decoration at
Praeneste. In the tomb a head (the so-called 'Ennius') marks **Plates 2, 3**
the Etrusco-Roman style in the early second century BC. But
Roman portraiture had also developed under Hellenistic
influence from Campania to present historical figures in their
own right, sometimes idealized in conception, often shown with
individualistic sharpness of features, 'warts and all'. It was no
new thing in Central Italy to give details of head, hair and
face, and the Roman nobles apologized to no one for their
physical features. They did not, however, have to lapse into
death masks, and Hellenistic 'realism' now made it unneces-
sary: the intensity of detail in Roman portraiture is distinguished by the term 'verism'. I illustrate this style from the Late **Plate 5**
Republic by the veiled head of an old man (presumably mak-
ing sacrifice). Alongside his stern ritualism I cannot resist setting the bronze head of the so-called 'Brutus' with its impression **Plate 6**
of moral seriousness. This is a difficult work, uncertain in
origin and date: perhaps Etrusco-Roman from the late fourth
century BC, or later in its idealized form, especially if we sense
the grave Roman, as indeed the Renaissance would have done.
The historical portraits of the Late Republic, with their associated coins, will appear later in their context.

The Roman coinage leaves no doubt of its traditional significance. About 269 BC the first issue of silver didrachms, following Greek models of the south, showed the Roman gods in bold
portraiture. Hercules' labours, for instance, had taken him to **Plate 7a**
Italy: from Etruria down to Magna Graecia he was worship-
ped, not least among the Latins; Rome recruited him and
established his cult at the Ara Maxima in the Forum Boarium,
where he stood to help her travelling merchants. At the same

Plate 7b

Plate 7c

Plate 7f

Plate 7d

Plate 7e

Plate 7g

Plate 7h

time Rome could boast her foundation as the city of Romulus and Remus, twin sons of Mars, suckled by the she-wolf. The combined theme was designed to impress the southern Greeks. Mars himself, the chief Italian god next to Jupiter, might attend on Roman policy and recall the Greek associations of Ares, wearing a crested Corinthian helmet. Then what deity could Rome cite better than Diana, the goddess of the Latins and their political league, whom the Romans had settled on the Aventine? She spoke for the central region of their power, in her 'Phrygian' helmet. Later tradition called up Janus, who watched both ways—one can do this with two faces—at the city gate, a great god while his duty continued; and along with him Jupiter himself, the city's ultimate protector, armed with thunderbolt and carrying his sceptre in his four-horse chariot; they made a fitting pair for a Roman coin. Then 'Roma' herself appeared, wearing her helmet; she was escorted by the chival-rous lancers, Castor and Pollux, the saviours of Rome (p. 110).

One might write dryly about Roman religion and its ritual, which the Romans practised with scrupulous care. Polybius did not believe in it, but he saw its effect. The fear of the gods, he remarks, kept the people in check and hindered corruption, in financial matters: a Roman's oath was his bond. But he misunderstood—as we may do—the function of symbolism in temples and statues; he underestimated the Roman feeling for a balance of nature in which divine forces and human activity worked together for good or ill: oracles and augury could thus be significant, unnatural prodigies were a warning that demanded expiation. The basic conception of deity was 'act' rather than 'personality', the play of functional spirits, develop-ing the primitive 'animism'; this gave scope for sacrifice, prayer, and ritual observance—as well as strict conduct. Worship evokes symbolism, and the Etruscans and Greeks had shown how to 'personalize' it in formal ceremony and monumental art, especially where deities like Jupiter and Vesta had assumed civic prominence; but we shall let the illustrations indicate this trend. One need only stress the complex view of cosmic order, the *pax deorum*, which could be maintained by the means by which tradition proved Rome had gained her power. If peace were disturbed or threatened, it must be restored to equilibrium —even by violence; that is why the ritual of declaring a 'just' war (through the priests known as *fetiales*) was adapted to the diplomatic 'ultimatum' for overseas warfare.

The sceptical reader will now be impatient, but there is more to say. Ritual is seductive: it may take the credit for success, and the Romans were superstitious and successful; their rites became formalistic, covering legalistic diplomacy and imperialistic policy, susceptible to unscrupulous exploitation. Polybius lived to doubt the Romans' 'good faith', and we have studied the social revolution that changed the conditions of public morality. The internal politics of the Late Republic made cynical and shameless use of the religious conventions—until Caesar, head of the state cult though he was, brought them down to earth. Yet we should keep the historical perspective; for Roman Italy would preserve much of the old belief, and Augustus made patriotic appeal to it.

Roman art illustrates the traditional ceremonies. I show part of the frieze of what is called (dubiously) the 'Altar of Domitius Ahenobarbus': the stiff reliefs of a formal occasion—with regret for omitting a graceful panel that depicts the wedding procession of Neptune and Amphitrite and attendant Nereids. Seated at the left with his tablets an official takes down information from three citizens, while two soldiers stand by and musicians play to the central scene. Here is Mars himself by the altar, and a toga-clad figure pours a libation. The sacrificial animals are led up—the bull, ram and boar of the *suovetaurilia* sacrifice—followed by two soldiers and a knight. The occasion? It has been taken as a demobilization of troops, but the presence of Mars and the soldiers does not necessarily make an army

Plates 8–10

scene. The Roman people, as in the Comitia Centuriata, carried a military organization of classes and centuries into their civic assembly. The frieze looks more like a scene of the census formalities, *viz.* registration of the people and public sacrifice, keeping the martial character of Roman citizenship in mind. It can hardly be coincidence that the Nereids recall the Temple of the Nymphs, where the census records were stored; the date is mid-first century BC.

Against this severe relief we may set a triumphal monument, in Hellenistic style, which probably celebrates Sulla's success in Greece during the First Mithridatic War (88–85 BC).

Plate 11 Between candelabra two Victories support a laurel wreath around a shield displaying the eagle of Jupiter over his thunder-

Plate 12 bolt; then we have a decorated cuirass and two trophies of armour flanking a shield that holds the helmeted head of 'Roma'. The strength of detail recalls the sculpture of Perga-mum, the clear composition is Neo-Attic in effect, and the work illustrates a fresh stage of Greek influence that appeared at Rome in the early first century BC, under Sulla. By this time, too, it became the fashion to place hard Roman heads on heroic Hellenistic bodies. The style was fused, and about 75 BC we see

Plate 13 the 'Roman general' from Tivoli. Standing (now on one leg) by his cuirass, he has an idealized Greek figure: his features are 'veristic' Roman, softened a little in the Hellenistic manner.

Plate 14 Meanwhile the ancient traditions survived in a relief of Mettius Curtius, who in response to an oracle (we are told) rode his horse fully armed into the chasm of the Lacus Curtius that had opened, ominously, in the Roman Forum. The monu-ment is an Imperial copy of a Republican original, probably adorning a balustrade round the Lacus Curtius; it is still represented *in situ* (by a modern copy) near the Column of

Plate 15 Phocas in the Forum. We also have—from a funeral urn prob-ably of the second century BC—a procession of knights, three pairs, following musicians to a shrine, where an attendant holds the sacrificial victim. Does the scene represent the solemn yearly review of the Roman *equites*? Perhaps this is to conjecture too much: it may be a funeral procession; but it still has social significance. Society was freer under the Late Republic, and wholesale trade had its place. The tomb of M. Vergilius Eurysaces, a wealthy contracting baker, still stands by the Porta Maggiore in Rome. It is firmly built, like a huge oven, on piles and coupled pilasters, its decoration playing boldly with the effects of light and shade. The reliefs illustrate the trade. Using a long scoop a slave bakes the bread, the dough already kneaded and rolled on two tables; the grain has been sifted, washed, and ground; I pass over the last stage of weighing before delivery. I also omit the time-worn funeral stele of Eurysaces and his wife Antistia.

Plate 18

Plates 16, 17

SOCIETY AND LITERATURE

The Etruscans had left their mark on Rome in religious practice and civic ceremony and transmitted Greek influence not only to Rome but to Latium, notably at Praeneste. The Republic kept these associations even after the Romans gained political independence, and Etruscan technical skill and art continued to influence the life of Latium. Rome rose to power as a Latin city, through diplomacy as well as war. Some of her leading families, too, were Latin in origin, and they preserved their local connections, which must have promoted her first treaty arrangements. Through South Latium and by sea from Ostia Rome had easy contact with Campania and the Greek civilization of the south. For all her insistence upon political hegemony the relationship, in cultural terms, was mutual. That is why Appius Claudius about 300 BC could organize the city efficiently and give it an Italian setting. Only the desperate struggle with the Samnites roused the impersonal brutality of militarism, after which we have to recognize the dichotomy of policy and culture. But the personal factor remained, and the spoils of con- quest in Southern Italy and Sicily, and later in Greece, brought Greek art to men who already knew it, through their Italian associations. It is false to speak of a rustic 'peasant' attitude in Rome; for peasants do not found empires. Like the Persians before them and the Prussians since them, the Roman nobles were landed gentry who made a profession of war and politics: rural but not rustic, socially conservative, they applied their ability to administration, in their own traditional terms. We have studied their weakness under the changing conditions of success. Yet *Realpolitik* does not exclude personal culture: it only restricts it to the leisure of a ruling class. The Roman aristocrats accepted Greek influence for themselves where they denied it to the general public.

The first Latin writers were not Roman born. Livius Andronicus from Tarentum, Naevius of Campania, Ennius and his nephew Pacuvius from Brundisium: when these men translated the variety of Greek literature into Latin, they were simply bringing Magna Graecia to Rome. Plautus and Accius from Umbria and Caecilius from Cisalpine Gaul drew on the Greek culture of Italy, and Terence from Africa could follow them. By the second century BC Rome was exercising the attraction of a metropolis. We have to recognize that traditions we call 'Roman' belonged largely to Etruria and Latium and touched Campania on the south. Hercules had laboured in the West. There, too, Odysseus had wandered—through the Scylla and Charybdis of the Straits of Messina to meet Circe at Cape Circeii—so let Livius Andronicus translate Homer's *Odyssey*. Aeneas from Troy had sought a home in the West, from Sicily to Latium, where his memory had long been honoured: if he visited Dido in Carthage, then let Naevius give epic back- ground to the First Punic War. Romulus had set Rome on her path of divine destiny, so Ennius could carry the *Annals* of the saga down to his own time. In the midst of their other writing these poets gave the Roman nobles a literary tradition which set Italy, and above all Rome, in the ambit of Mediterranean civilization; they could do so because they felt that culturally Rome and Italy were now one. Meanwhile the capital city enjoyed Plautus' bold adaptation of Hellenistic comedy to Latin conditions. When Roman senators began writing history they used Greek, as Gibbon might have used French, to be in the fashion of historiography: their own circle could read their work as well as the Hellenistic public. Cato turned to Latin, but he only gave Italian colour to a Greek pattern in his *Origines* of Italy. By the late second century BC two trends had emerged: first, the regular use of Latin and the rise of Roman scholarship, secondly the confident borrowing of Greek rhetoric to improve Latin composition and style; but we should appreciate by this time the integration of Italian culture.

Cultural progress was only as free as the noble patrons would allow. The Magna Mater helped to expel Hannibal, but she had to limit her orgiastic rites. Dionysus was a powerful god in Italy, but Rome brought his 'Bacchanalia' under regulation. Greek philosophy looked too clever for the Roman youth: Cato might have enjoyed Socrates' talk but he would not have let him into the Forum; so the Senate in the mid-second century BC checked Epicureanism, banished philosophers and rhetoricians from the city, and hustled home the Athenian philosophers, Diogenes, Critolaus and Carneades, as soon as they completed their official business on an embassy. Drama was in fashion, but not with the dignity of a stone theatre: Pompey broke through this restriction. Hellenistic portraiture in public statues was closely controlled. At the same time Polybius moved among the nobles, and the Stoic Panaetius added ethical considerations to the claims of traditional morality: the nobles felt that these men contributed to their own way of thinking, as they had accepted the Italian writers of an earlier generation. We see a strong tradition leaning against a storm of change.

Individualism would break in to give life to Latin literature—one thinks of Catullus and Lucretius—yet the old standards of judgement remained. Cicero applied them in Italian terms, while Sallust quoted them to make a case for the emergence of new talent. Finally Augustus and his writers—Virgil, Horace and Livy—combined personal sentiment with the traditional conception of Rome or, rather, Roman Italy to sustain the best of what the Republic had to offer. We must set this develop-ment in historical perspective; meanwhile we have to show the monuments of Republican Rome and the archaeological evidence of Italy.

CHAPTER VII

Monuments of Republican Rome

FORTUNATE the student of Rome who approaches the city by air: his eye will teach him the conditions of her early history as he flies into Fiumicino, if only his imagination grasps the human effort that was devoted to the problems of security and defence. The great semicircle of Southern Etruria and Latium lies below, a dim green, bounded on the clear horizon by the encroaching hills—a region that challenged its people to look after themselves. In weakness it tempted raiding or invasion; in resistance it demanded leadership, unity, and organization; in strength it urged expansion across the strategic passes and settlement to control them. The Romans responded to the challenge and developed habits of policy that brought them power in Italy and empire in the Mediterranean. We have to survey the monuments of their first success.

THE TIBER AND OSTIA

The Tiber winds a tawny course to the sea, navigable to its Roman crossing, where the local hills rise slightly from the Latin landscape. Far to the north stretches the coast of Etruria: we shall find Rome founding the colony of Cosa in the terri, tory of Etruscan Vulci, and closer the site of Caere (modern Cerveteri), the Etruscan city that would be most closely asso, ciated with Rome; inland lie the remains of Veii, whence Etruscans dominated the Tiber valley above Rome and pressed their influence to the sea. Caere and Veii played their part in Roman history under the Tarquins: from Veii came Vulca, the sculptor of the Capitoline temple. Our task is to show how the Roman Republic broke free of the neighbouring Etruscan power and learned valuable lessons in doing so. In 396 BC

Rome destroyed Veii, strong and wealthy, in a siege which later historians likened to the siege of Troy—an inverse comparison, since Rome traced her descent from a founding by Trojan Aeneas! We can still see the remains of the temple of 'Apollo', the wall that Camillus undermined to take the city, and—more significant for the future—the gate and roads connecting Veii with the rest of Etruria; for though the Etruscan cities acted freely in a loose confederation, they kept their communications, and the Romans would borrow their engineering technique in road-building. Rome's great talent lay in organizing the inventions of others.

Plates 19-22

Flying into the airport one glimpses Ostia, which used to stand at the mouth of the Tiber: now it is inland, separated from the sea by the Tiber's silt deposit, and the river has partly changed its course. Whether or not the early king Ancus Martius founded Ostia or the Romans made much of its salt beds, the Tiber mouth was essential to Rome. About 350 BC a fortified post—the Ostian 'castrum'—was established there, on a rectangular area some five acres in extent, fronting the Tiber; it was built in tufa stone, roughly shaped in oblong blocks, which survive in part to confirm the date. Ostia was the port of Rome for overseas shipping, but—until the Emperor Claudius built his harbour—it was an open roadstead. Vessels of shallow draught might proceed up-river to Rome, using oars or by towline to the bank, while the larger ships would berth or discharge their cargo by lighter; thus Ostia developed landing facilities and storage space, and river transport—Tiber barges—connected it with the Roman quays and warehouses. The rise of Rome as a Latin and Italian capital carried Ostia with it; the Second Punic War increased its importance; and Roman relations with the West during the second century BC made the port, in effect, a part of Rome itself, as Puteoli on the Bay of Naples became Rome's port for her Eastern shipping. Ostia was enlarged by further building, until in the Sullan period new walls surrounded more than 170 acres, and the town plan continued into Imperial times. But as the Tiber mouth silted up, fresh facilities were provided near at hand; so we have to concentrate our air view, looking at the forum area, Plates 23–25 which represents the 'castrum', and its ancient masonry.

From Ostia we move up the Tiber stream to Rome—safely now, through the flat land which the malarial mosquito once seized from the declining capital. If civilization means drain, age, we must not pass the great drain of ancient Rome at the Forum Boarium. The Cloaca Maxima still discharges usefully Plate 26 into the Tiber: it is protected by a modern embankment, but older views show its outlet. Along the line of a watercourse it drained the valleys between the Roman hills, running through the Roman Forum to the Tiber bank. The Cloaca Maxima, indeed, was the making of Rome. Canalized at an early period —one thinks of Etruscan engineering—it was arched over by the second century BC and kept in repair, notably by Agrippa in 33 BC.

Let us follow Roman tradition farther upstream to the S, shaped curve of the Tiber, where the Tiber Island marks the historic crossing. The Island itself, readily fashioned into the form of a ship by the first century BC, was dedicated to Aescu, Plate 27 lapius, the Greek god of healing: he came from Epidaurus in Greece after Rome had suffered a plague in 293 BC, and his sacred snake chose the Island for his shrine—now represented by the Church of San Bartolomeo, just as the saint also founded St Bartholomew's Hospital by the Thames. There were Republican bridges to the Island: the Pons Fabricius of 62 BC (improved in 21 BC) from the city side, still preserved, and the Pons Cestius of the same period crossing to the right bank. Below the Island the Pons Aemilius of 179 BC—the piers supplemented by arches in 142 BC—provided a single crossing, and one arch survives. Farther up the river, we may note, the Pons Mulvius carried the main northern road, the Via

Flaminia of 220 BC; stone arches of its rebuilding in 109 BC by Aemilius Scaurus are still to be seen.

Going north in the city towards the Piazza Navona and Pantheon we reach the point from which an air view of the central plan of Rome shows the Republican setting: the photograph looks obliquely south to catch the distinctive shadows. From the Campus Martius by the river one glimpses the Island and, to the left, the area of Capitol and Roman Forum as far as the Colosseum. Though Roman building since Augustus has overlaid the Republican remains with marble, the old order is still visible. The visitor, however, is more likely to base himself on the Capitol; so I give a sketch plan—it relates the modern thoroughfares to the ancient sites—from the south in order to orientate the serious walker in the north-western area.

TIBERSIDE ROME

In the Late Republic the dominating feature of the Campus Martius was Pompey's theatre, built in 55 BC as Rome's first stone theatre. A magnificent structure, its façade comprised a series of arcades adorned with half-columns, Doric, Ionic and Corinthian as the eye moved upwards, and it was decorated lavishly with marble and stucco. An adjoining portico gave shelter to the gathering spectators: here or near at hand was the Curia Pompeii where 'even at the base of Pompey's statue, which all the while ran blood, great Caesar fell'. Few earlier nobles, even had they the wealth to do so, would have favoured glorifying the stage to the extent of corrupting over 10,000 citizens at a time! Sentiment changed, and Pompey had seen what a Greek theatre of this kind could mean in Mitylene; but he satisfied Italian tradition as well as his own pride by making the tiers of seats in the auditorium run up like the steps of a temple—rather like the arrangement at Praeneste—to a shrine of

Plate 28

Fig. 14

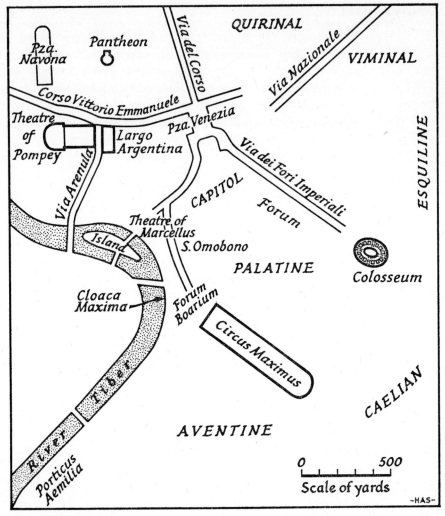

Fig. 14. Guide to Rome

Venus Victrix. The Roman emperors from Augustus onwards kept the theatre in repair. Today we have only some of its vaults —one can dine under them—but it has left its outline on the modern street plan; I illustrate this from an air photograph.

Plate 31

About AD 200 the Emperor Septimius Severus set up a marble plan of Rome, the *Forma Urbis*: it survives only in fragments, which have to be pieced together—like a defective jigsaw puzzle—in the light of the archaeological evidence. These

Plate 30   fragments indicate part of Pompey's theatre and portico, along with two temples, one a distinctive round building. The site

Plate 29   lies in the Largo Argentina, where the foundations of four Republican temples have been uncovered. There is as yet no evidence to identify these temples: the gods must be content with capital letters (A–D). But temple C—the nearest in my illustration, looking north—dates from the fourth century BC, with fragments of terracotta revetment. It follows Italic fashion at the back of a high podium (platform), built of *grotta oscura*, a yellow tufa quarried near Veii, and the masons' marks recall those of the 'Servian' wall, which we shall be describing. Temples A and B correspond to the indications of the Severan plan; and perhaps the podium of the round building (B) may belong to the infamous Curia Pompeii.

Some forty years later Augustus followed Pompey's fashion by building the Theatre of Marcellus, the conspicuous remains of which—topped by Renaissance work to become the Orsini palace—mark the way back to the Island. Near-by a temple of

Plate 33   Apollo the Healer is represented by three marble Corinthian columns, reconstructed from fragments found on the ground; they date from a restoration by C. Sosius about 33 BC, but the temple was dedicated as early as 431 BC after a plague in Rome. It was to serve Apollo for four centuries, until Augustus also honoured the god on the Palatine in thanksgiving for his victory over Antony and Cleopatra at Actium. Alongside stood a temple which, it is believed, C. Duillius dedicated in 260 BC, during the First Punic War, to celebrate his famous naval victory against Carthage off Mylae in Sicily, Rome's first great success at sea. We know its remains from AD 17 as a temple of Janus, restored by the Emperor Tiberius; but it has Augustan foundations; perhaps Duillius originally built his temple to Portunus, the god of shipping.

We have been in the old Forum Holitorium, the vegetable market, and now we enter the Forum Boarium, the cattle market, which lined the Tiber bank below the Island. This was an archaic area of habitation, as the oldest remains show, joining the Forum Romanum through the Velabrum, under the western Palatine face; for the Roman hills always looked towards the Tiber. Populous and busy as it supplied the rising city, the Forum Boarium kept its religious monuments. When the records indicate over a dozen temples here it is not easy to identify the archaeological sites. I have not shown the three temples that are absorbed into the church of S. Nicola in Carcere, one ascribed to Juno Sospita, another to Spes; but the sacred precinct of S. Omobono lies open to view. Here we see the foundations of two temples, separated by a portico, one of them still under the present church: they are now ascribed to Fortuna and the Mater Matuta, goddess of growth. In the Forum Boarium itself—above the course of the Cloaca Maxima—there are two standing temples. The rectangular Ionic temple nearer to the Tiber, a monument of Hellenistic fashion on its Italic podium, was once identified as the temple of Fortuna Virilis, while the adjacent round temple with its Corinthian columns—built of marble on a tufa podium with Greek steps—was ascribed to Vesta (yet round temples do not all belong to her!) or to Mater Matuta. Now they are shrines to unknown gods: the student of Republican architecture need only admire them and note that the old attributions are some/times still used.

From the fourth century BC the Tiberside was organized for shipping. Light warships lay at their yards, alongside a tufa mole, while Ostian craft berthed by their quays. We have already viewed the port of Ostia. Its imports brought to Rome such essential products as grain from Sicily, wine and oil from

Plate 32

Plate 34

Campania, and timber—bulky cargoes that were most cheaply transported by sea. Eastern goods landed at Puteoli were brought by coastal shipping to Ostia and Rome. The Tiber developed its own lighters and barges, which could be towed up-river to the capital. During the second century BC there were important building improvements in the Tiber *emporium*. In 193 BC the city aediles Aemilius Lepidus and Aemilius Paullus erected a large market hall with access to the river, the Porticus Aemilia, and in 174 it was rebuilt. This magnificent warehouse had fifty stepped barrel-vaults, carried on arches to make parallel departments and approached by arcades. Part of the portico wall remains: it was built in concrete, covered by the irregular small stonework of *opus incertum*; this is evidence for the dating of early concrete construction in Rome. More warehouses were added, such as the original Horrea Galbana, and the whole area marked the growth of the Roman capital in trade and commerce.

Plate 35

By the same principle we turn to the Roman aqueducts. A great city needs not only to import cheap food but to maintain its supply of pure water. Rome drew upon the inland springs of Latium and built aqueducts to carry their water for distribution in the city. In 312 BC Appius Claudius had constructed the Aqua Appia, in 272–269 the Aqua Anio Vetus added to the supply; but neither shows conspicuous remains. During the second century BC, as we have seen, Rome increased its population, and in 144–140 the Aqua Marcia was built. Drawing from Subiaco it ran for fifty miles underground, in Etruscan fashion, except where it crossed gullies on arched conduits, as the earlier aqueducts had done; then it rose on arches for some seven miles to enter the city at high level and distribute its supply from a reservoir near where the Baths of Diocletian would stand. A splendid structure as it approached Rome, its arches were later used to carry also the Aqua Tepula (125 BC) and the Aqua Julia (33 BC) into the city on its back. I show

the Marcian stonework earlier in its course at Ponte Lupo and Plates 36, 37
illustrate the triple entry of aqueducts into Rome near the Porta
Maggiore; for we are treating not only Rome's public health
but her functional architecture.

We return to central Rome and its Republican city-wall, the
'Servian' wall, traditionally ascribed to the king Servius Tullius. Enough of the masonry survives at various points to show
the line it followed in protecting Rome's hills by a continuous
circuit: one need only step outside the Termini railway station
to see an impressive stretch. The evidence, however, suggests
something more complex than the traditional account. If
Servius Tullius built the defences of the regal period, they comprised probably an earthwork *agger* which—in the early Italic
way—supplemented the natural advantages of the site; any
stone revetment was in the local grey *cappellaccio* tufa. In 390 BC
the Gauls proved that these defences were inadequate to stand
a siege. The main part of the wall, in fact, consists of *grotta
oscura*, cut in squared blocks and set without mortar (*opus
quadratum*); I have illustrated it with a view that includes a Plate 38
cross-section. The material and technique point to fourth-
century construction, and the masons' marks appear to be
Greek, as if experienced Sicilian workmen had been employed;
also, Livy reports that the censors of 378 BC let out contracts
for the building of a wall in squared stone. We may conclude
that the Romans determined never to be caught by any Gallic
invasion again, and the 'Servian' wall as we see it embodies
their policy. Their alliances and the foundation of colonies
enlarged their strategy of defence, but the wall—patched at
weak points—saved them from Hannibal. When it was
strengthened again—by later work that included the use of concrete—we have to think of the civil war that Rome brought on
herself in Italy; Sulla, for instance, probably reinforced the
city's fortifications in 87 BC and placed artillery (military cata-
pults) in the arched casemates that flank the main gates.

THE ROMAN FORUM

From its prehistoric heights the Palatine commanded the Tiber and surveyed the ancient growth of the Forum Boarium, then it turned to support the Tarquins' Capitol in dominating the Roman Forum. Centuries later it would support conspicuously the Imperial court. Both its first and its last importance lie outside our Republican period, but it never lost its traditional and religious significance. During the Second Punic War Hannibal drove the Roman people to despair in the strength of their gods, and they extended their scope of appeal for divine assistance. Let Greek gods, then, be recruited, since they had their place in the world order and many had already joined Rome. In 205 BC the Sibylline books directed the Senate to the Magna Mater of Pessinus in Asia Minor, great mother of the gods. An embassy consulted the Delphic oracle and went on to Pergamum, where Attalus gave them the black meteor stone of the goddess and a ship to carry it with due solemnity to Rome; the young Scipio Nasica of the Cornelian family was judged worthy to receive her. The stone lay—as a hint to the goddess—in the temple of Victory on the Palatine, until she should have her own shrine. Magna Mater did her duty, and Hannibal left Italy. But she had her own interests, too, and the startled Romans awoke to find eunuch priests celebrating her orgiastic rites. The Senate imposed its discipline upon the cult, and consecrated a temple to Magna Mater on the Palatine in 191 BC. After a fire in 111 BC it was rebuilt by Q. Caecilius Metellus in 109 and restored again in AD 3. Today its slight remains mark one of the quiet places of Rome.

Plate 39

There is now no Capitoline temple of Jupiter to lift the west/ward skyline of the Roman Forum. The splendid Etruscan building of the Tarquins has left parts of its massive sub/structure, and architectural study has reconstructed its plan, while terracotta fragments suggest the character of its decoration;

for its appearance we have to rely upon literary references, later
coins, and argument from Etruscan analogy. The temple was
embellished under the Republic, but in 83 BC it suffered a dis-
astrous fire. Q. Lutatius Catulus rebuilt and dedicated it in 69,
and Augustus renovated it. It was burnt during the civil war
of AD 69 and again, after Vespasian's rebuilding, in 80; then
Domitian restored its magnificence for the rest of the Imperial
period. Only the substructure continued throughout its history
to the present day.

Fig. 5

Apart from a glimpse of Victor Emmanuel's monument,
recalling likewise a united Italy, our eye is held by the Tabu-
larium—or rather, since Michelangelo's time, the Senatorial
Palace—and below it the columns of Saturn's temple and the
Imperial Rostra. A closer study of the Tabularium reveals the
fine squared masonry of the strong substructure and the first
story with its arcading and Doric half-columns. This was the
building that Q. Lutatius Catulus erected in 78 BC to house
the state archives: the Roman writers took a records office for
granted, but two inscriptions have preserved its identity. Even
its rear façade, as we can see, was designed to add to the monumental impression of the Forum in Sulla's period. Saturn may
have had his shrine from the first years of the Republic, and a
temple probably about 400 BC, but the remains of the high
podium belong to a rebuilding by L. Munatius Plancus in
42 BC, and the prominent Ionic columns to the early fourth
century AD. The god was no mere patron of 'Saturnalian'
revelry: his temple contained the Roman treasury in its vaults,
entered by a door (still with lock-holes) near the temple stair-
way; here officials handled the cash and financial documents of
the state. To the right stood the Temple of Concordia, which
Camillus founded traditionally in 367 BC to celebrate peace
between the patrician and plebeian orders, and L. Opimius
rebuilt it in 121 BC after Gaius Gracchus' death; its remains
are Augustan (Aedes Concordiae Augustae).

Plate 40

To the right of our view lay the Comitium, the meeting place of the Roman people, in front of the Senate House, and between Comitium and Forum stood the Rostra, providing a platform for the Republican orators. The name is taken from the ships' prows of Antium with which C. Maenius in 338 BC, probably building the first stone structure, decorated the side facing the Forum. The glory of the Republican Rostra speaks for itself in Cicero's orations; we may omit the archaeo-logical details of its foundations. What we see before us is a modern restoration of the Rostra after Caesar's replanning of the Forum and Augustus' work moved the platform westwards (Rostra Augusti). The glory had departed, and Imperial decisions were taken on the Palatine.

Fig. 15a

Let us take two views of the Roman Forum from the Pala-tine side. The first looks towards the Tabularium, past the Corinthian columns of Castor's temple (Temple of Dioscuri) in the foreground and the Senate House of Diocletian at mid-distance on the right. Castor and Pollux, the Dioscuri, twin sons of Zeus, the heavenly horsemen, had appeared in Southern Italy to help Locri against Croton and then—according to tradition—they came north to intervene at the battle of Lake Regillus in 496 BC and support Rome against the hostile Latins, and they watered their horses at the Lacus Iuturnae in the Forum. Thus legends are adopted; but the Romans estab-lished a cult of the Dioscuri as early as 484 BC, probably under influence from Tusculum, and the twin brethren took over the ceremonial parade of the Roman knights. The temple of Castor was restored by L. Caecilius Metellus in 117 BC, rebuilt by Tiberius in AD 6, and renovated a century later; for the Dio-scuri were saviours of Rome.

Plate 41

The Republican Senate House, where Roman senators sit-ting like kings issued their decrees to Italy and the Mediter-ranean world, lives—like the Rostra—more in history than in material remains. The ancient building must have undergone restoration: we know at least of Sulla's work in 80 BC, a fire in 52, and reconstruction by Faustus Sulla. Caesar began a new building with a fine oblong hall, the magistrates' dais facing a central door, the senatorial benches of marble on either side; and this plan was preserved: we see it in the surviving structure as restored by Diocletian. The power of the Senate had gone. Even the building has been salvaged from the medieval church of Sant' Adriano. Its bronze doors are in St John Lateran.

Our second view from the Palatine extends across the Forum to the temple of Antoninus and Faustina (AD 141), now adapted as the church of San Lorenzo in Miranda, with its portico of six Corinthian columns. Before us lie the shrine of Vesta, partially reconstructed, on the left, and between it and San Lorenzo—on the Sacred Way—the foundations of the Regia. Political places may change, but a holy precinct keeps its original site and plan. A marsh, a market, an Imperial city's centre, the Forum preserved its main traditions throughout its monumental development, especially where family, state and religion were bound together in common ritual. Vesta was the goddess of the hearth, an intimate part of the home and then— through association with the royal household—no less a part of the state, even when the kings had left. Her round shrine perpetuated the prehistoric straw hut of the Palatine, with its central hearth and smoke vent, and the Vestal Virgins tended her pure eternal fire, first under the king and then under the high priest (*pontifex maximus*) of the Republic. The remains we see are Augustan, with some architectural fragments from a restoration about AD 200; but the shrine was early and it had suffered from flames less gentle than Vesta's fire. Towards the Palatine the Atrium Vestae gave residence to the six Virgins; its visible structure dates from reconstruction after the fire of Nero (AD 64).

Alongside Vesta's shrine on the Sacred Way—and surely by design—stands the Regia, 'the king's house'. It has the

Plate 42

Fig. 15b

a   b

Fig. 15. Roman Forum

(*a*) *Denarius* (c. *47 BC*), *reverse. Rostra, with magistrates' chair above, ships' prows below, PALIKANVS.* (*b*) *Denarius* (c. *57 BC; Q. Cassius*). *Domed temple of Vesta, on left voting urn, inside magistrate's chair, on right tablet inscribed AC* (absolvo, condemno)

ancient orientation of the precinct and its plan was scrupulously preserved: a hall with central hearth, approached by two ante-chambers and flanked by a walled courtyard that contained its storage pit and well. Its stone remains go back to the fourth century BC, when Rome made good the Gallic devastation of 390 BC, and to restoration after a fire in 148 BC, not to mention a rebuilding in marble by Cn. Domitius Calvinus in 36 BC. Here the Pontifex Maximus of the Republic exercised his authority not only over the neighbouring Vestal Virgins but over everything in Rome that called for the sanction of the gods —in effect, most official business—and kept his archives, which would play their part, as we have seen, in Roman historio-graphy. His residence lay eastwards on the Sacred Way, close enough to the Atrium Vestae to be joined to it after Augustus. The Vestal precinct with the Regia now survives modestly, as it always stood with due modesty; but we need look no further for the powerful influence of Roman tradition.

So much, then, to illustrate the significant monuments of the Republican city, and we may sum up historically with an impression of the Roman Forum from the Capitol: I give a profile sketch to aid our discussion. The picture is complex.

Plate 44

Fig. 16

First let us—with respect—dismiss the later Imperial additions, except as landmarks: along the left the *Umbilicus Urbis* (the city's central point) and the Arch of Septimius Severus, not Diocletian's Senate House which restored that of Caesar, but the buildings which stretch from the Temple of Antoninus and Faustina past the Arch of Titus (closing the eastern part of the Forum) to the distant Colosseum. On the far right the Palatine broods over the Forum again; the buildings at mid-right, covering the way to the Forum Boarium and Tiber, may be ignored, as also the Column of Phocas in front of us. For the rest one can talk about Republican Rome.

We need not glorify the Roman Forum. The Romans cele-brated the triumphal processions that moved along its Sacred Way to the Capitol, and they suffered there the political dis-orders of the declining Republic. Let us rather visualize the evolution of this significant place. Once the ancient Palatine looked out over a marsh: before our eyes the Lacus Curtius   Plate 14
recalls it—a legendary spot with a Sullan pavement—while the Cloaca Maxima still drains it into the Tiber. Then the Romans   Plate 26
raised their citadel on the Capitol, with its great Etruscan temple and lesser buildings devoted to the state, and the tradi-tional Tarpeian Rock of public execution. We are in the Tabu-larium, which marks their administrative care. Below us stand Saturn's columns, near Concordia's temple foundations, and   Plate 40
farther to the left is the Carcer Mamertinus, the state prison, with its domed circular chamber of the Tullianum. Septimius Severus' arch blocks our view of the old Comitium and Rostra, lying between the Senate House and Forum—the centre of Republican freedom, near the archaic monument of the *lapis niger*; the Senate House and Rostra, as we see them now, show the siting of Caesar and Augustus. It was here that Republican Rome developed her political life.

The Forum drew the city to itself. Below us leftwards, between Senate House and Basilica Aemilia, the Argiletum joined it with the eastern part of Rome; to the right the Vicus Iugarius led to the Tiber, and farther on, beyond the Basilica Julia, the Vicus Tuscus—surely recalling the Etruscan days—indicates the way to the Forum Boarium. The Sacred Way moved through the Forum from the east—the landmark is Titus' arch—forking at the Regia to proceed to the Capitoline slope. At mid-distance we have the evidence of civic develop-ment in the early second century BC, when Rome realized itself as the Italian capital. Once a common market growing around traditional points of worship it now became the administrative centre of a commercial world. The butchers, for instance, had disappeared—on our left—to the area where Caesar and the emperors would follow them in establishing their fora. Business became larger, and it needed buildings that would serve its pur-pose. The Greeks had proved what regular planning could do in their city centres, for utility and decoration, through the arrangement of colonnaded porticoes: the Romans coordinated their work for more direct control, and this duty fell to the censors in the Forum. In 184 BC Cato founded the Basilica Porcia above the old Comitium. We can see—beyond the Comitium—where M. Aemilius Lepidus and M. Fulvius Nobilior, censors of 179 BC, followed his example. The Basilica

Fig. 3c

Aemilia was restored in 80–78 BC—a coin illustrates its columns with their shields—and rebuilt in 55–54 at Caesar's expense by L. Aemilius Paullus and dedicated by his son in 34 BC. With shops and a colonnade opening upon the Forum it was a handsome structure, in its latest stage notable for an historical frieze, and it kept the Aemilian name until Rome fell. On our right Ti. Sempronius Gracchus, censor of 169 BC, who should be remembered more in his own right than as father of the Gracchi, established the Basilica Sempronia. Caesar would replace it with his Basilica Julia: we have its pavement and piers, giving the ground plan, and the piers presumably sup-ported two stories. The earlier basilicas must have owed their

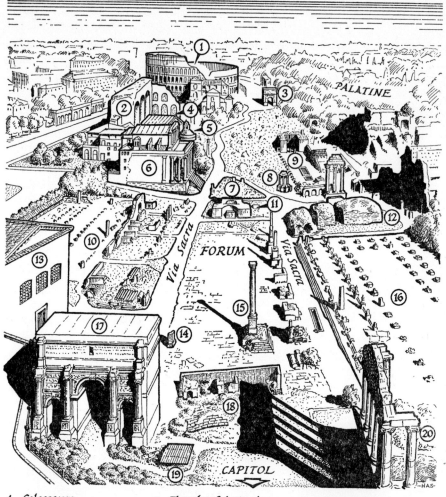

PALATINE

FORUM

Via Sacra

Via Sacra

CAPITOL

1 Colosseum	6 Temple of Antoninus	13 Senate House
2 Basilica of Maxentius	and Faustina	14 Lapis Niger
or of Constantine	7 Regia	15 Column of Phocas
3 Arch of Titus	8 Temple of Vesta	16 Basilica Julia
4 Part of the Forum of	9 House of the Vestals	17 Arch of Septimius Severus
Peace	10 Basilica Aemilia	18 Rostra
5 Temple of Romulus–	11 Temple of Caesar	19 Umbilicus Urbis
(so-called)	12 Temple of Castor	20 Temple of Saturn

Fig. 16. Sketch of Roman Forum

construction already to the use of concrete and the application of vaulting, which allowed a high building, with good light, ing, to meet the needs of varied activity. In any event we may visualize them as places of commercial transaction, legal decision about disputes, and the social gathering that attends business affairs. The dates are worth noting. Fifteen years of evidence (184–169 BC), overlaid but significant, illustrate the revolution in Rome's social history that we have analysed in economic terms.

Tradition kept its place in the course of material progress; for the Romans respected the relations with the gods that had brought them to power. In the open Forum the Lacus Curtius was permanent, along with a statue of Marsyas, a fig tree, olive and vine. More important, the holy precinct of Regia and

Plate 42

Vesta's shrine on the Sacred Way was preserved as the focus of Roman religion, and 'the Pontifex with the silent Vestal ascended to the Capitol'.

Plate 41

From their temple near-by Castor and Pollux continued to watch over the safety of the city. The Romans would add from their own number to the heavenly host. Looking down the Forum we see just short of the Regia the remains of the Temple of Divus Julius, dedicated to the deified Caesar by Augustus in 29 BC, on the spot where the people had rushed to 'burn his body in the holy place'. In front of the temple stood a platform, its rostra decorated with ships' beaks from the Battle of Actium, which contained in a semicircular niche the altar that commemorated Caesar's informal cremation. Between Divus Julius and Castor the Arch of Augustus celebrated Actium and displayed the Fasti (chronological lists) of consuls and of generals who had won triumphs; the fragments (in the Capit, oline Museum) help us in following Rome's course of govern, ment and war. The monuments glorifying Caesar and Augustus in a sacred setting show how Venus' Julian descen, dants might reclaim the right of dynastic rule!

The Forum has disclosed the stages of its history. The second century BC brought functional development to its middle area, the Sullan period added monumental ordering to its Capitoline end; Caesar reviewed its arrangement in orientation and detail —from Senate House and Rostra to the Basilica Julia—and enlarged its activities to the Forum Julium; and Augustus completed Caesar's plans. Later emperors would maintain its glory, despite dilapidation and fire, until the Goths and Van dals plundered Rome. Yet the Roman Forum did not perish by foreign violence: it was quietly picked to pieces by medieval builders with their ox-carts and limekilns.

What of the Romans who thronged there in the Republican heyday? Wealthy nobles had their great houses, some on the residential Palatine, where Imperial building has spared a few remains. The people lived in varying comfort, many with little, as the city struggled to support its growing population. Urban pressure raised high tenement buildings over the *tabernae* of shops and workshops, especially in the crowded quarters near the Roman Forum and the Forum Boarium, much as one can see in Trastevere today. The tenements were built at first in timber framing with mud bricks or wattle and daub, then by the second century BC in concrete construction: the *insulae*, which we know from Imperial times, especially at Ostia. Such Republican building was expendable and replaceable, so we find no trace of it under the medieval and modern city. We shall do better to look elsewhere in Roman Italy for the material evidence of private life.

CHAPTER VIII

Archaeological Evidence for Roman Italy

ROME'S MONUMENTS catch the eye and the Roman authors focus attention upon the city, but we have to take an Italian perspective. The literary evidence, when it is pieced together from the references of historians, antiquarians and such technical writers as Vitruvius, can be supplemented by archaeological study, especially if this is interpreted in topo-graphical context. Since 1945 the systematic excavation of various sites, wider surface exploration, and the use of air photography have produced a more general picture than was possible earlier. Not only the classic sites of Pompeii and Ostia but other places can now be compared with one another as well as with Rome, in the light of common features and local differences, against their background and development. The Archaeological Institutes in Rome have added their efforts to the work of Italian scholarship, and the enterprise has opened up a new field in the social history of Roman Italy; we shall discuss, for instance, the evidence for town-planning and the 'centuriation' of land surveying.

Let us begin with Rome's opponents, since her historians tended to damn their memory. The destruction of Veii had eased Etruscan pressure on Rome, but Etruscan influence left its mark in Latium. Praeneste, for example, once an Etruscan outpost, held its position as a leading Latin city against Rome until the Latin League was dissolved in 338 BC, and then it became an important Roman ally. Its art shows its men in bronze: two men carrying a third ('the fallen comrade') make a decorative lid-handle for a bronze 'cista', the coffer that held articles of toilet use, from the mid-fourth century BC.

Plate 45

The Gauls of Northern Italy, as we have seen, had sacked Rome in 390 BC and they continued to threaten Etruria and Latium until the late third century BC. In 225 they launched a major attack. At Telamon on the Etruscan coast the Romans were fortunate to crush them between two armies. The bronze figurine of a Gallic spearman (late third century BC) found near Rome represents one of these fierce warriors, with horned helmet and Celtic torc and belt. The Gauls reinforced Hanni-bal on his arrival in Italy, and the Romans fought heavy cam-paigns in the early second century BC to subdue the tribes and develop Cisalpine Gaul. The Samnites, disputing with Rome the control of Central Italy, were her most bitter enemies; they roused and suffered the brutal execution of her militarism. Samnite soldiers would serve Rome without forgetting their past. Later, when she spurned their claims for recognition, they would turn their arms against her again in the Social War (91–88 BC)— and Sulla would repeat the Roman revenge; for next to Hannibal the Romans had feared the Samnites. I show a formidable warrior in archaic armour, wearing the helmet fitted for crest, bronze breastplate with bosses, belt and greaves —probably of the fifth century BC.

    Plate 46

    Fig. 19

    Plate 47

Under these conditions, then, Rome was not the only city of Latium or Southern Etruria that looked to its defences in the fourth century BC and replaced the old earthwork *agger* by a complete stone circuit like the 'Servian' wall. Indeed, the Latin cities had first to defend themselves locally against Rome and the neighbouring hill tribes and then, even under Roman leadership, to guard against the danger of external attack. Norba, for instance, which as a Latin outpost lay close to the Volsci, kept its military importance. I show the massive walls and defensive gateway of the fourth century BC; the city developed the chessboard planning of the Roman period. In Southern Etruria we see the strength of fortifications that were still necessary there in the third century BC at Roman Falerii.

    Plate 48

    Plate 49

The Faliscans, once holding a high point at Falerii Veteres above the Tiber in association with Veii, had entered into alliance with Rome in 293 BC; then Rome forced them to move to a near-by site at Falerii Novi, where they built lofty walls over a small gateway for local defence, within a system of communications that bound them to Rome. The Via Amerina ran through the new city, affecting its town plan, while the great north road of the Via Flaminia passed on the east, both serving a larger area and driving ruthlessly through a land-scape which the older Etruscan roads had followed more gently. We owe our present knowledge to the work of the British School at Rome in Southern Etruria.

COLONIES

Rome extended her control of Central Italy by founding colonies. There were two types by the textbook. 'Roman' colonies, established along the coast on Roman public land, consisted of 300 citizen families which had garrison duties. 'Latin' colonies were larger, planted more widely at strategic points and designed to promote their own municipal life, where Latin rights would be sufficient, even for the Romans who joined them. The distinction was, in fact, a functional one, related to the purpose and prospects of the settlement. Later, when Rome had to secure Northern Italy, her citizenship was more generally valuable; then we find large 'Roman' colonies which could make their own local life. So much for the politi-cal formula: we can now also use archaeological evidence to study the planning of the 'Latin' colonies. First let us define the problem of Roman town-planning. As we have noted in the *Fig. 13* 'Polybian' camp, it involves the principle of chessboard arrangement, where a city has parallel streets (*decumani*) cut at right angles by cross-streets (*cardines*) so as to form blocks of building, ranging from civic sites to humble domestic housing.

The factors of planning involved first terrain, then policy, power and technical skill, all variously interrelated according to the historical development of the place. Early defence uses the natural features of a site, while internal organization is unsys-tematic, except for ritual purposes. Commerce adds its require-ments, with shops, warehouses and markets, until civic policy takes charge. Planning depends upon the power to dictate policy, which is never easy in old-established cities. Then tech-nical skill, *e.g.* in concrete construction, allows further advance. New foundations at a later stage of development will benefit from the immediate coordination of these factors, and the Romans were able to impose a policy on land and people.

Town-planning was not a new thing in Italy. Etruscan ritual had given a formal city centre and quartering of the area within the walls, while Etruscan influence must have encour-aged Italic trends towards more regular arrangement; but this does not explain the systematic Roman development. The Greeks by the fifth century BC had evolved geometric planning along 'axial' lines, as suited the prominence of their religious and civic building. This led to the coordination of chessboard planning; their work was followed in Sicily and South Italy, and the famous Hippodamus of Miletus, we are told, applied its principles at Thurii in 443 BC. Certainly the Italian Greeks had the civic enterprise and freedom, under favourable condi-tions of terrain, to promote their town-planning: their sites prove it, and Naples may represent it today. The Etruscans could have learnt it, if one argues from the early remains of Marzo-botto. In any event from the mid-fourth century BC—one thinks of Ostia—the Romans were in a position to follow not only the Etruscans but the Campanian Greeks. We must not, how-ever, regard Roman town-planning as simply derivative. The variable conditions of topography and politics in Central Italy called for positive action to plan functionally, and this was Rome's achievement.

Plate 25

COSA
Fig. 7

In 273 BC Rome founded the 'Latin' colony of Cosa in the territory of Etruscan Vulci to hold the coastal area; it was reinforced in 197 BC, with further civic building, but lost its importance towards the end of the Republic; thus one has definite Republican evidence. Excavation under the auspices of the American Academy at Rome has shown the principles of planning. Cosa was strongly situated on a promontory overlooking its harbour; the harbour, subject to shifting sand blockage, was kept clear by tidal sluices and later by breakwaters. The town (covering some 33 acres) was protected by polygonal walls, with eighteen towers and three main gates, in an irregular circuit that fitted the lines of natural defence; its water supply was maintained by cisterns. Within the wall ran an ambulatory street—vital for defence—and the city was laid out in a chessboard pattern of streets, which defined the blocks of housing. In the north-eastern angle of the central crossing lay the forum,

Plate 50

at the southern point of the city stood its Capitol. Our air view looks over a housing quarter past the forum area towards the sea. The forum was at first a simple site, flanked to NE by the Comitium, Curia, public hall and magistrates' offices. In the early second century BC this part was rebuilt monumentally so as to provide a basilica, which—like those in the Roman Forum—opened on its long side to the forum; the Capitol received a new temple, and the forum a triple arch at its main entrance. In its Imperial decline Cosa's basilica became a

Plate 51

theatre and the adjoining public hall an inn. I show a ground view of the remains of the basilica, with the theatre additions, facing the forum. These details illustrate how Rome extended her organization in Central Italy, through military and civic building, administration and municipal development, in the third century and confirmed it in the second century BC.

ALBA FUCENS
Fig. 17

Across Latium from Rome the 'Latin' colony of Alba Fucens was founded in 303 BC during the Samnite wars to secure the strategic communications of the region; the Rome–Tibur road

was then carried through to this new point as the Via Valeria, and the site has revealed its 68th Roman milestone. We owe our recent knowledge to joint Italian and Belgian excavations. The remains are more complex in rebuilding than those of Cosa, but they show the same early plan. Situated on a three-point hill-top at the foot of Mt Velino the colony was defended by an irregular circuit of polygonal walls, with four gates, adapted to the terrain. The more level ground in the middle, after some terracing, was laid out in a chessboard pattern. The Via Valeria shows a right-angled turn into the city, where it forms the main NW–SE street through the civic area. At the central crossing we find in its northern angle the forum—its earliest buildings superseded—and in the eastern angle a basilica presenting its long side towards the forum and backed by a temple and round market. These buildings represent the monu-mental development we have noted at Cosa, here from the Sullan period; as regards the basilica in its civic setting the architectural reader may refer to Vitruvius' account of his work at Fanum (V, 1, 6–10). I illustrate Alba Fucens in an air view   Plate 55
of the site from SE, looking along the Via Valeria to the civic centre; and at ground level a view across the market to the   Plate 54
basilica platform, with *tabernae* (shops) below, and Mt Velino in the background.

LATIUM

We return to Latium and the municipal progress of its cities under the influence of Rome; a map indicates their relation-   *Fig. 17*
ship. From the beginning of the Republic—if we may trust Polybius' dating of the first Carthaginian treaty—the Romans had aimed at controlling the south-western area. On building Ostia they set maritime 'Roman' colonies at Antium in 338 BC and Tarracina in 329 BC. But the social developments from the second century BC are now more important. I show the

Plate 52 great arched substructure of the temple of Jupiter Anxur at Tarracina, with its stone *opus incertum* covering concrete con-struction, as an example of Sullan architecture that kept the seascape in view. From the same period we have the high barrel-

Plate 53 vaulted nave of the warehouse at Ferentinum, above the *tabernae* entrances; it marks the effect of concrete building on market

Plate 35 halls that we have noted in the Porticus Aemilia at Rome.

Yet we must not underestimate the traditionalism of old Latin cities. They had resisted Rome, then joined her without loss of pride; their men served Rome and took her citizenship with honour; here under the Late Republic one finds the best Romans. Such cities made municipalities in their own right,

Plate 58 within the Roman context. I show the round temple of Tibur, the so-called 'Temple of Vesta', with its Corinthian capitals and Hellenistic frieze of the early first century BC; London readers need only visit the Bank of England to find a copy of the columns. It is usual to compare this temple with the round

Plate 34 temple of the Forum Boarium; we may observe the distinction between Latin treatment and the fashionable style of Rome.

Plate 59 Likewise Cora has the Doric columns of a temple of 'Heracles', which may be compared with the Ionic temple of 'Fortuna

Plate 34 Virilis' in the Forum Boarium as a blend of Italic tradition with the Greek orders of architecture, leading to the Imperial temples.

PRAENESTE   After its early Etruscan associations Praeneste's strong Latin traditions upheld the position of the city, with its oracular shrine of Fortuna Primigenia. It shared in the development of Latium, especially during the second century BC, and it suffered for its importance by sacking in the Sullan period of civil war; then its sanctuary was restored in an impressive piece of monumental design. The remains illustrate how Roman architecture now combined the Italic principle of symmetrical building along a main axis with the Hellenistic conception of planning to fit a landscape, and how the technique of concrete

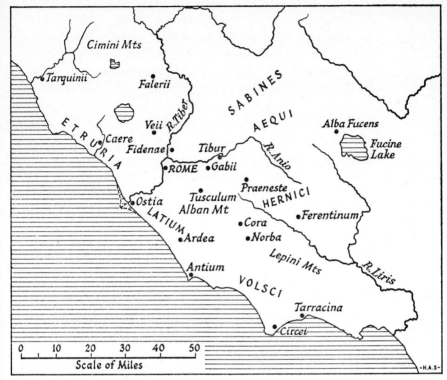

Fig. 17. Map of Latium

construction allowed flexibility in the use of vaulting, arches
and curved colonnades. The eye moved straight up the slope
of Praeneste from the formal entrance at the bottom to the
shrine at the top, passing an elaborate series of terraces with
their architectural decoration, but never losing its line. I show
an air view in order to give the setting, which comprises most
of the town, and a reconstructed model of the upper site. In the
lower area there were a temple (now part of the cathedral), two
caves that became apses of buildings, containing the Alexan-
drian mosaics of Praeneste; and between them a two-storied basilica, where an inscription preserves the name of M. Lucullus

Plates 56, 57

125

(consul in 73 BC, brother of the famous general). A two-level terrace—here our air view begins—was backed by a polygonal wall, which formed the base-line of the upper sanctuary. Ramps went up on either side—note the low triangular facing—to the next terrace, with its backing of columns and a balanced pair of semicircular niches (the 'hemicycles'). Another terrace, showing arches with half-columns, led to a square court bounded by a portico, and so to a semicircular area rising in steps to a portico through which one could see the circular shrine of the statue itself. This magnificent site speaks for itself: Rome was now living up to her cultural position as a Mediterranean capital.

POMPEII

It is not easy to treat Campanian Pompeii in broad Roman context, though the city flourished under the Republic. Let us dismiss—however regretfully—the buildings, the everyday things, and the human relics of AD 79, and apply archaeological study to the remains of its earlier history: even so, a problem persists—how far may one generalize in Roman terms about a Campanian city? Of course Pompeii became Roman in the sense that Italy became Roman, with the varied regional elements that, under Roman coordination, composed its civilization. But the Pompeian 'atrium' house, once studied as the 'Roman' house, how far was it typical? Partly, even in Ostia, but only where similar conditions of space and comfort allowed: not in the overcrowded 'industrial' quarters of Ostia or Rome, where people lived in the high tenement houses we know as *insulae*. We have to take a social perspective and use the comparative evidence that has come to light in other places.

Pompeii was an ancient Oscan settlement, which came under early Greek influence; it developed in its Greek setting under the Etruscan domination of Campania. During the Samnite influx of the fifth century BC it grew in population and civic importance. The oldest part around the forum shows two main streets crossing at the centre and an ambulatory rampart street. One can hardly speak of regular town-planning before the city expanded to north and east, presumably to accom-modate the Samnites, and built the present circuit of walls; this was the period when Greek town planning first influenced Italy. Pompeii became predominantly Samnite, in language and administration, as part of the general development of Campania. Under Rome the second century BC brought in-creasing prosperity: the forum area became a monumental civic centre, and we have fine houses from this time. Joining the Italian side in the Social War Pompeii suffered by the settle-ment of veterans and was assimilated into the general pattern of Roman Italy.

An air view from the south-east shows the forum area: allow- Plate 62
ing for some Imperial building or restoration on the eastern side, it indicates the mid-second century BC reconstruction. The forum itself, one might say, lay open in Italic 'axial' symmetry within a Greek colonnade; but by now we should think of a composite Campanian style. The lower end of the forum was backed by the Curia and municipal offices; to its left the basilica presented its narrow side, opposite to the right was the Comitium. On the left again, above the basilica, the temple of Apollo maintained the god's occupation of the site from at least Etruscan times; I illustrate its steps, podium and surviving Plate 60
column, with its eastern colonnade. At the top of the forum stood a temple, where we now see the Sullan Capitolium dedi-cated to the Roman triad of Jupiter, Juno and Minerva. To the right, above the Comitium, the building of the Eumachia (a cloth market) and the Macellum (provision market), dating from the first century AD, continue the civic organization of the main trading quarter. Pompeii reflects the formal development of prosperous Italian cities from the second century BC to the

Sullan period and its remains serve to illustrate their town-planning.

We may also refer to Pompeii, along with Ostia, for evidence of domestic architecture and decoration—briefly and in terms of the social conditions. The Italic town house of any quality was built round a central court. In the Pompeian houses one entered through a vestibule into the 'atrium', an area partially roofed with an opening that admitted light and let the rain fall into a shallow trough in the floor (*impluvium*); I show the 'atrium' of the early 'House of the Surgeon'. The 'atrium' was flanked by rooms, and behind it lay the principal room (*tablinum*) with its side rooms in triple arrangement; at the back was an enclosed garden. The plan was symmetrical and func-tional, as suited the close family life of the upper classes. Such a plan, too, allowed elaboration in detail following Greek style, for instance, to use columns supporting the 'atrium' roof opening, and a portico—the 'peristyle'—surrounding the gar-den, with rooms behind it. We find this development in the wealthy houses of the second century BC, and I show the 'peristyle' garden of the 'House of the Vettii'. Ostia shows a similar trend; but Rome's sea port differed from the comfort-able Campanian city. In any event the poorer people lived in crowded houses or, as at Ostia, the pressure of population raised high tenement buildings (*insulae*) above the shops at ground level; even 'atrium' houses would turn their outer rooms into shops. As a rule—and we should not regret it—the *insulae* of the Republic were substantially rebuilt under the Empire.

A good house, enclosing its family, calls for interior decora-tion that will bring life to its walls, and Italian fashion bor-rowed from Hellenistic art. We classify Roman frescoes in the datable Pompeian styles, which seem to have general applica-tion. The 'First Style' of the late second century BC used painted stucco to give the appearance of marble panels and design; here I illustrate the painted 'atrium' of the 'Samnite House' in

Plate 61

Plate 63

Plate 65

Herculaneum. The 'Second Style' of the first century BC aimed at a stronger architectural impression and opened the wall, as it were, through magic casements into ritual or mythical scenes and fairy landscapes. This is varied art, running close to the Augustan period, and we may leave illustration to the works on Roman painting.

We can see the luxury of the Late Republic in the urban 'peristyle' houses, but we should not forget the 'portico' villas of the countryside or sea coast that brought comfort and elegance into the open air. This was an independent trend in architecture, for one could build freely to command a landscape or sea view and add the Greek colonnades and interior decoration. The remains are Imperial, since luxury keeps up with the times; but the fashion developed under the Late Republic, as we know from Cicero's circle. I cast back from a painting in the Pompeian house of Lucretius Fronto to show   Plate 64 what a maritime 'villa' was like. In the foreground a boat stands off a landing/stage; behind the first porticoes lie separate buildings among trees, against a background of rising hills. The picture illustrates what the wealthy families of Roman Italy sought in the planning of their 'villas'. Town and country were never far apart, and we may move north to Avezzano (near Alba Fucens) to gain an impression. A relief depicts the bird's/eye view of a well/built town behind a high gate   Plate 66 and strong walls, and outside it 'villas' standing in their land/scape; the work is from the mid/first century AD, but it repre/sents a Republican development.

AGRICULTURE

Urban life and agriculture, too, were closely related in their marketing. We have treated the economic factors of the second century BC: now it is time to consult Cato and apply the results of recent archaeological study. Cato set his typical farm be/tween Southern Latium and Northern Campania, where his senatorial contemporaries had best scope for investment in land. Although he praises farming for its traditional virtues, he has profit in mind and the regular use of slave labour, while his instructions could serve an absentee landlord; but he clearly knows what he is talking about. Let us take his advice about crops in his order: a vineyard, an irrigated garden, willows (for basketry), an olive grove, a meadow (for fodder), grain, trees (for stakes), an orchard, oaks (the acorns for pigs); and we know that he recommended grazing (for meat, leather and wool). One should look for land, he says, that would support this kind of production. A farm of this kind could sell wine and oil, vegetables and meat, leather and wool, while its other products supported its operations. What type of farmstead was necessary on the estate? Cato gives instructions about building; we cannot discuss them in detail, but I am able to illustrate the first discoveries of Republican remains.

In Cato's Campanian area, on the present Villa Francolise site near Capua, the two 'rustic villas' of Posto and San Rocco are being excavated. They date from the Republican period, Posto from the end of the second century BC, San Rocco from the mid-first century BC; they were rebuilt on a larger scale under Augustus and again in the late first century AD. At Posto the Republican villa, set on its platform of squared stone, has a square courtyard, containing wells and an oil-separating vat: on the left a timbered portico, at the back the residential part, to the right the slave quarters—in what seems a typical

Plate 69

plan. I illustrate the oil-separating vat. When the olives had been ground from their stones and the pulp crushed, the mixture was run into a vat, where the watery fluid sank to the bottom and the oil could be skimmed off. We see here the hollow floor where the water could settle and a stand from which to do the skimming. The lead pipe fed a well, sealed off with a tufa cover; the open well, however, is Augustan. San Rocco is not

Plate 68

yet fully plotted. We can see the main terrace, on the left a

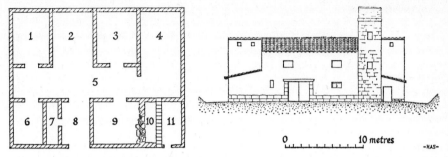

Fig. 18. Plan and (conjectural) elevation of Villa Sambuco (late second century BC). Rooms 1–4 storage rooms; 5 corridor; 6 stable (?); 7 stairwell; 8 entrance; 9 slaves' quarters; 10 tower; 11 toolshed. Upstairs manager's quarters

retaining wall, at the back a revetting wall against the hillside, which bounded the Republican building; a main room with Republican mosaic faced left; the rest is largely later restoration. A dark triangle low at the left side points to a bedroom: it had a floor of ground limestone, inset with black points, and a mosaic panel (towards the back) outlined the position of the bed; in the front, however, the meander pattern (over a cut-down wall) is Augustan. So much for an impression, and we shall learn more from these American excavations of the first archaeological evidence for Cato's account.

Plate 67

In Southern Etruria at the Villa Sambuco—near San Giovenale, NW of Veii—Swedish archaeologists have excavated a Republican farmhouse; it dates from the late second century BC and lasted well into the first century AD. I reproduce C. E. Östenberg's plan and conjectural elevation. The living quarters were modest—this is no 'portico' villa—while the storage space was large enough to hold quantities of oil, wine and grain that would go to market. We see, in fact, a working farm, which the owner operated through a manager and slave establishment—typical, we may assume, of the small estates that now played their part in the economy of Roman Italy.

Fig. 18

Roman policy had regularly practised 'close settlement' on the land, in the 'Latin' colonies, for instance, or sometimes by individual allotment; and the Gracchan agrarian reforms and the later planting of veterans extended the system. Air photo-graphy has now revealed its details, as crop-marks reflect the technique of 'centuriation'. Where an area was taken for redis-tribution, the Roman surveyor moved in with his *groma*—a standing rod that supported two horizontal bars at right angles, with plumb-lines suspended from their ends. The *groma* orien-tated two intersecting axial roads; in parallel alignment with these roads the area was divided into square (or rectangular) sections, separated by field tracks, so as to form a grid pattern like that of town-planning. The standard section was, theoreti-cally, the *centuria*, a square of 200 iugera (about 125 acres) to hold 100 family plots; but the surveyor could adapt his system to the conditions of the ground. So much, briefly, on a complicated matter: we have to examine the evidence from the air.

Cosa and Alba Fucens, one may note, had 'centuriation' in their countryside, and so had stretches of north-western Cam-pania where there was 'close settlement' on the land. But let us look southwards to Apulia. Near Lucera I show Republican 'centuriation'—think away the central inclined airstrip. We can see the traces of field divisions, vineyards and olive groves: the arrows indicate small farms flanking a double-ditched 'cen-turial' road. Alongside this road another view gives a farm in more detail: observe the break in the ditch (A) for approach to the farm, and the entrance (B) to the ditched farm enclosure; the circular crop-mark belongs to a prehistoric compound. At low left (C) we have the lines of vine-trenches in the farm's vineyard. Here at ground level there appear the dark earth-filled streaks of vine-trenches cut in the limestone subsoil. Then the excavated part of another farm shows, to the right, the front patio and, on the left, twin oil-refining tanks. We have moved from economic organization to personal living and labour, and the evidence illustrates the local variety which soil and market-ing imposed upon Italian agriculture.

Plate 70

Plate 71

Plate 72

Plate 73

Chapter IX

Revolution and Reaction

REPUBLICAN ROME, it is said, collapsed under the weight of military success, because her 'city-state' institutions were unequal to the political consequences. True, perhaps, in constitutional terms—but this is to neglect the human factors of policy. *Moribus antiquis res stat Romana virisque*, wrote Ennius, who saw the interplay of men and traditions in Rome. Quoting his words Cicero would lament a mutual decline: 'Our traditions once produced great men, and great men maintained the traditions. Now we have lost the colour and even the outline of the picture. The traditions are forgotten, for we lack the men. It is our crime that the state stands only in name' (*Repub*. V, 1). Why? Power, it is also said, tends to corrupt, and militarism raises dangerous arts that turn inwards on the people. Yet this, too, does not explain the social and political complexity of the Late Roman Republic.

ADMINISTRATION AND POLITICS

Rome was no simple 'city-state'. She had expanded her policy to include first Latium and then the rest of Italy, and to co-ordinate their manpower and resources. It was as the leader of Italy that she had conquered the Mediterranean. The nobles used their wealth and social patronage to gain office, but their work developed in systematic skill. These men were professional in mind: they turned experience into a school of administration. We find this, of course, notably in the military sphere. The levy of citizens and allies for the army, as Polybius describes it, rivals any modern method of conscription, the training of troops was strict and technical, and the overseas campaigning was conducted on a sound logistic basis of support.

No general took the field without capable staff officers, many with longer experience than himself, and good soldiers had a career well before Marius. Further, we should realize, legions stood permanently in the provinces that needed defence or control, while the levy kept them up to strength. There were 'standing' armies, in effect, under the Republic for regular duties: that is why Augustus would so quickly establish his military system.

In Rome itself, as the city became the Italian capital, we may glance at the administration of private law. The ancient 'customary' law had been set down in the Twelve Tables (450 BC), as a basic statute; this involved a system of rights of action (*legis actiones*), and it supported a rigorous formalism in legal practice. Such procedure may dispense rough justice while social conditions remain constant, and the city praetor (*praetor urbanus*) could extend its application by edict. About 242 BC Rome's Italian connections encouraged the appointment of another praetor (*praetor peregrinus*), whose duty it was to judge cases involving non-citizens engaged in Roman business. In the second century BC, as all commercial routes of the Mediterranean led to Rome, the old practice of the 'civil law', however liberally the praetors interpreted it, could expand no further. There were too many cases which under the new conditions raised principles of 'equity', and 'equity' required a more flexible procedure to assist the praetorian jurisdiction. The Lex Aebutia changed the situation: it gave the magistrate power to take wider considerations into account, beyond the limits of the strict 'civil law'. Then the praetors' edicts (*ius praetorium*) had greater influence upon the growth of Roman law, jurists added their counsel, and Rome met the legal problems of her imperial place.

So far, so good—and we have seen something of Rome's quality. But, as the critical reader must surely be asking, what of the provinces? And why the heavy hand on Italy? We shall examine provincial policy later: the Romans for too long regarded it in terms of 'occupation policy' rather than 'colonial government'. As for Italy, where we have discussed the Senate's methods of adapting the old treaty relationship to the need for integration (p. 84), it is now desirable to let events speak for themselves. One general comment is worth making. The Roman rulers, like many sound administrators, were better at developing precedent than they were at rethinking such problems as those of Italy or evolving new principles of provincial policy. They were inhibited by their own social and political training.

The Roman nobles assumed their own traditions and authority. Looking back Sallust said: 'An oligarchy managed affairs at home and in war: it held the treasury, the provinces, public office, and military glory' (*Jug.* 41). In effect, the noble families provided the majority of higher magistrates and domin- ated the Senate, once by public merit, now largely through inherited influence. They were subject to a special form of electoral temptation. Their urban clientship became more dependent on their subsidy; so 'pay a dole and claim a vote'. Wealth was as necessary as reputation in winning popular support, whether in personal connections or through spectacu- lar public entertainment, 'bread and circuses'. A crisis might rouse the people to acclaim the man of the hour— only too often the eleventh hour! But there was no regular way open to talent, unless—by birth or under patronage—a man had noble back- ing, financial advantages, or an exceptional opportunity of gaining distinction. At the same time the field of talent was increasing.

Below the senatorial class in the income brackets that deter- mined the political structure of the state the 'equestrian' class had its place: the *equites* were men of substance, as carefully registered by the censors as were the senators themselves. One might call them the upper 'bourgeoisie', who tend to emerge in revolution against an aristocratic regime. Some were business-men, the *publicani*, undertaking Rome's public works. Others were landed gentry, the upholders of local government in the country towns: they had prospered, but they preserved the old-fashioned standards of public morality, while Rome itself degenerated. Why should their sons not rise in the state? The 'equestrian' class, then, had two faces: one shrewd and sharp, the other serious and respectable, both showing a glint of am-bition. The business group resented the Senate's control, but they were well set to exploit the profits of empire; the gentry must have deplored the narrowness of political oligarchy, and they stood ready to help broaden the system of Roman rule. The 'equestrian' name covered two functions, and we should not let the history books—whether Roman or modern—obscure the distinction.

By the mid-second century BC Rome was paying for her lack of constructive policy. The Spanish tribes had yielded to the strength and diplomacy of Sempronius Gracchus, but they would not tolerate misgovernment and arrogance in his suc-cessors. In 154 BC the Lusitanians revolted and fought until 138, when they lost their leader Viriathus; the Celtiberians joined them for a short time and then fought again from 143 until 133 BC, when Scipio Aemilianus crushed them at Numantia. M. Claudius Marcellus could have settled this rebellion as early as 151 BC, had the Senate been ready to accept anything but surrender. Meanwhile conditions in Macedonia allowed the rising of Andriscus, which was crushed in the Fourth Macedonian War (149–148 BC), and conditions in Greece encouraged the Achaean League to defy Rome: in 146 BC Mummius destroyed the ancient city of Corinth. In North Africa trouble between Carthage and the expanding power of Numidia brought Roman intervention in the Third Punic War (149–146 BC), and Scipio Aemilianus destroyed Rome's old Phoenician rival, root and branch; we know of the Senate's intransigence and duplicity in this war. Why should the Senate have treated two great civilized cities so barbarously? Perhaps militarism had reached its brutal extreme; yet the question is more complex, if we accept the indications that Rome was no longer capable of supporting rationally the strain of widespread revolt within the short space of five years.

PROBLEMS OF CHANGE: THE GRACCHI

The Roman army still relied upon the old citizen levy, and citizens qualified in terms of property for the duty of service. The qualification might be reduced, but economic changes had reduced the number of property-holders on any terms; and those who were qualified could ill afford to hazard their livelihood. Special campaigns to plunder rich cities like Corinth and Carthage, with the help of siege artillery, were one thing: it was another to march against the formidable Spanish tribes through rough country. Colonial warfare needs regular troops. Roman citizens were liable for 'call-up' during sixteen years—not, however, for continuous service. We may agree that two periods of five years' service is enough for one life-time! The Romans settled for six years at a time. In hard campaigning the troops must be experienced and have confidence in their generals and officers; but the Spanish wars were disgracefully conducted. No wonder, then, that the levy was unpopular, especially when unhappy generals attempted to recall veterans into service. It was an original right of tribunes of the plebs to defend private citizens against official injustice: they now intervened in the levy, even to the point of imprisoning consuls. The Senate lost a century's control of men and methods at home—temporarily perhaps, but the spell was broken, and the recovery of tribunician initiative in personal problems might reopen the way to radical legislation. To make matters worse urban prosperity was receding, and the proletariat—now swelled by landless

men and foot-loose veterans—suffered under depressed conditions. Gang slavery provoked a major uprising in Sicily during
the years 135–132 BC. Like Appian (*Civil Wars*, Bk 1) we
shall treat the Gracchan period in its Italian perspective.

Already Scipio Aemilianus' group had proposed a policy of
land resettlement, but Scipio hesitated to provoke disturbance
in Italy. Another powerful group under Appius Claudius
Pulcher was bent on similar reform in order to restore the military system. Tiberius Gracchus, Claudius Pulcher's son-in-
law, brought aristocratic authority to his tribuneship in 133 BC.
He had not only the army but the condition of the people in
mind—by old traditional standards, not limited by the recent
precedents for senatorial control; and the momentum of events
carried him into plebeian action. His agrarian commission
applied a programme of close land settlement to Italy. At what
political cost? There are two items. First, by appealing to the
people against the veto of his fellow-tribune, M. Octavius, and
by deciding to stand for re-election, he prevented the nobles
from direct obstruction and the tactics of delay: they resorted
to violence and informally killed Gracchus. Secondly, the
Italian leaders saw their communities losing land which they
had farmed for three generations—for the benefit of unwelcome
Roman settlers. So this was the reward for their long cooperation! If the Senate could not keep the bargain, then they
had better demand Roman rights for themselves. Scipio
Aemilianus eased the situation, but disillusion is not simply
forgotten. As tribune in 123 and 122 BC Gaius Gracchus kept
these problems in view. First, he brought the 'equestrian' class
into play. The *publicani* were allowed to contract for the
collection of taxes in the new province of 'Asia', the kingdom
of Pergamum lately bequeathed to Rome; from the whole
class, including the landed gentry, he proposed to add to the
Senate but had to be content with giving them judiciary rights,
in particular on the court dealing with cases of provincial extor-

tion. Secondly, surveying the Italian scene, he proposed to extend Roman citizenship at least to the Latin states. The programme was polemical but, in the light of developments, logical—therefore the more threatening to the oligarchy. One murder may be casual, a second needs excuse. The nobles, led by Opimius, adapted the emergency powers of the Senate to the domestic challenge and—by the 'ultimate decree'—they formally killed Gaius Gracchus. When Opimius was prosecuted, his acquittal saved their case. Two bold tribunes and a dozen years had challenged the old regime; but the Senate survived, and the nobles after 120 BC might dismiss the crisis as a passing episode.

It is important to forestall generalization about Late Republican politics at this stage: we must at least wait for Marius and Sulla, and preferably learn from Pompey and Caesar. Yet it may help to define the potential factors of the situation. The Gracchi had probed the oligarchy's constitutional defences in the Senate, but the tribunician position could not withstand the sally of 'emergency powers'. A consul and tribune in alliance might do better, but Marius and Saturninus were defeated. Sulla used his army to gain control and restore the Senate's authority, but his action supplied another precedent for violence. The Romans drew a distinction between 'Optimates' and 'Populares', as if the state were divided in rival parties. The 'Optimates', it is true, comprised the leading nobles and their adherents, exploiting the prerogatives of the Senate; the 'Populares' were neither 'democratic' nor a group: they were ambitious individuals—often free-lance nobles—who used the consulship or tribunate to take their policies directly to the popular assemblies. The people? Rome's electorate was now unsteady and by habit corruptible, certainly unrepresentative of the Italian state that had emerged under Roman rule. The distinction of 'Optimates' and 'Populares' was one of procedure in exercising government over the people, as between dictatorial 'advisory' authority and aggressive 'executive' power. Why the dichotomy of constitutional functions, which even in tense relationship need not be incompatible? The people had lost their basic strength. Yet we may not hark back to any 'Polybian' balance of functions. Constitutional incompatibility is the mark of a revolutionary situation. Republican Rome lived under a struggle for political power: the nobles fought to retain their position, their opponents attacked it. But the struggle was conceived in narrow terms, while its setting became larger. The 'equestrian' class with its bourgeois aims, whether in commerce or government, would claim a place. An extension of Roman citizenship in Italy might broaden popular representation in the assembly and even in the Senate. The impact of external events, as Rome headed for trouble in the Mediterranean, would stress the need for talent. The situation, in effect, was more complex and serious than the Roman politicians were ready to grasp. We have to study its shifting pattern not under conventional labels but in the real terms of power and problems.

MARIUS TO SULLA: ITALY

The Jugurthine War in Numidia (112–106 BC) raised up Marius, a fine professional soldier from the gentry of Central Italy. He had attached himself to the noble Metelli—a coin shows their family elephants drawing Jupiter's chariot!—and moved to the consulship of 107 BC. It was then that he reformed the army system so as to accept long-service volunteers without property qualification, a revolutionary decision that simply concluded the earlier trend. The threat of the northern Cimbri and Teutones to Italy (113–101 BC), once the senatorial generals had failed, kept him in successful command as consul re-elected continuously from 104 to 100 BC: the victories of Aquae Sextiae and Vercellae saved Rome. The Roman people

Plate 77a

acclaimed Marius, but the nobles envied his glory. How then could he carry the political measures to settle his retired veterans? Not through the Senate, with its arts of obstruction, but directly by the people's vote—assisted by an able tribune, who could prepare the political ground. The logic of events led Marius and Saturninus to revive the Gracchan procedure against the oligarchy, this time in greater strength. Yet the key to Late Republican history is to appreciate the skill of the nobles: they split Marius and Saturninus, and regained their initiative—just as fifty years later they would bring Pompey and Caesar into the arena.

We must not follow Rome in neglecting Italy for this critical period. The historical tradition is now summary in form, often too loosely stated to explain the complex development towards the Social War (91–88 BC). Yet the issue is a central one and its interlocking factors need definition. The uprising, for instance, was not general: the Latins stayed out. The Italian states would hardly have moved, had their leaders not changed their view of Rome. Italy was more socially integrated; but there were regional differences in the spirit of revolt, perhaps reflecting attitudes—one thinks of Samnium—that survived from past history. To make these points is simply to ask questions, and we need more local information, especially where archaeological exploration may throw light on the social conditions. Let us attempt to trace a pattern. The Latins had prospered in their Roman environment and they enjoyed personal association: their magistrates became *ex officio* Roman citizens, their young men could make a Roman career. Likewise Etruria and Umbria were content in their old relations with Rome. It was different in the Samnite country. The rural communities of Central Italy saw Rome in the character of travelling magistrates or unwelcome settlers on local public land. Their own rights were still important to them: if these rights failed, then they would demand the equality of Roman citizenship. The Greek cities of Southern Italy, especially since their people were also doing business in the Aegean, under Roman administration, looked for the full protection of Roman law.

The Italian authorities had cooperated with Rome—despite increasing difficulties—because this bolstered their own position. The arrangement was only as durable as its advantages. After the shock of Gracchan land policy, the Senate's recovery restored confidence. Yet the 'equestrian order' now complicated the political situation: the *equites* had influence at home, their financial members pursued interests in the East, and they held legal power in the courts. Then the rise of Marius—for all his encouragement of Italian soldiers—and the revival of Gracchan policy by Saturninus can only have upset the Italian leaders again. How far would the Senate keep its part of the Italian bargain now? The Italians knew their Romans. That is presumably why they crowded in Rome to support their case. When the consuls of 95 BC expelled them, they might suspect the worst. When the Senate in 91 BC prevented M. Livius Drusus from extending the Roman citizenship, they drew their own conclusion and went to war. The Social War—as the

Fig. 19a, b

coins illustrate—saw a resurgent *Italia* and the Sabellian bull of Central Italy trampling the Roman wolf; it closed with Rome and Italy united in common citizenship, the Roman citizenship now defined in broader terms. One might celebrate

Fig. 19c

the imperial future of 'Roman Italy'; yet there were still the facts of Roman political life. The Italians could benefit immediately in their legal position—but what of the political effect? This would depend upon their voting power: it was 'one tribe, one vote' in the main legislative assembly of thirty-five 'tribes', regardless of the size of the 'tribe'. How fairly would the Roman government implement the extension of citizenship in its distribution of the new citizens throughout the 'tribes'? That would depend upon the group that controlled Roman

Fig. 19. Social War (*a*)–(*b*) *Italian denarii of the Social War* (c. *90–88 BC*), *reverse*
(*a*) *Italia wearing helmet, seated on shields, crowned by Victory,* ITALIA. (*b*) *Sabellian bull trampling Roman wolf; Oscan lettering* (villetif = Italia). (*c*) *Denarius* (c. *69 BC*), *reverse. Italia* IĀ *holding cornucopiae, with caduceus* (*herald's wand*) *behind, meeting Roma,* RO, *with spear and foot on globe;* CORDI

policy; the nobles had a poor record in point of Italian enfran-chisement. The first distribution of Italians in the 'tribes' was not representative, and they had an interest in the condition of Rome's internal politics.

The Social War had raised up new generals of differing political character. Alongside the old Marius and his supporters there were such men as Sulla, champion of the Senate, and Cn. Pompeius Strabo, first of the warlords, who would launch his son, Pompey the Great, on his career. Military success now made for political influence, because veteran soldiers already attached professionally to their generals would carry their per-sonal loyalty into retirement: the land settlement of veterans extended the scope of 'military clientship'. The common dan-ger of the Social War had checked the struggle between Marius' group and the nobles; now it broke out again, in the setting of Italian politics and external events. We have to con-sider the effects of the First Mithridatic War (88–85 BC). Mithridates VI of Pontus had challenged Rome's position in Asia Minor by occupying the province of 'Asia'—once the kingdom of Pergamum—and invading Greece. Sulla, the

Plate 77b

143

Plate 77c

Plates 11, 12

consul of 88 BC, was appointed to command against him. In legislating for fairer treatment of the Italians the tribune Sulpicius Rufus also proposed to supersede Sulla by Marius in the Eastern command. Sulla led his legions on Rome to seize control, then he left for Greece. Marius' group recovered power by violence, and sent their army to the East; I show a unique coin of the general Fimbria. Two Roman armies against the same enemy and each against the other—to display Roman policy! Was this the moment of truth for Republican Rome, if rival armies should decide her fate? Not strictly, unless civil war became regular; but it means that we should think more about the factors of power than about constitutional tactics. Sulla drove Mithridates out of Greece—we may have his triumphal monument (p. 94)—and imposed peace in Asia Minor; then he took over Fimbria's army and returned to Italy. His 'Marian' opponents gathered strength against him, with Samnite re-inforcements, and Sulla had to fight his way to the very gates of Rome, before he entered to take charge of the Roman state.

SULLA'S POLICY

During ten violent years we have seen—in the sharp outlines of the situation—how the Republic's divided policy in Rome and Italy, hardened by the brutal use of armies, moved to the point of civil war. The oligarchy and its rivals had carried Roman militarism to its logical end of turning on the state: certainly, even when we allow for personal enmity and mis-judgement, the issues mark a revolution in the political and social tradition. Now Sulla held the field and he was deter-mined to restore the old regime, organized to meet the new conditions. By vote of the Comitia Centuriata he became 'dictator legibus scribundis et reipublicae constituendae', that is, 'dictator for the redrafting of the constitution'. In terms of precedent Sulla's office joined the emergency powers of the ancient dictatorship with the legislative functions of the Decemvirate of 450 BC; in effect it created a new position of supreme authority, limited in time only by his own view of the critical need for it. Aristocratic in style and confident of his personal destiny, 'L. Cornelius Sulla Felix' vested his dictator-ship with the regal ceremony of a Hellenistic court; but his policy remained conservatively Roman, and he would retain office only for the length of time he took to carry out his pro-gramme of legislation. First by the 'proscription' (outlawing) of his 'Marian' enemies and the confiscation of their property he crushed the remnants of opposition and was able to settle his veterans on the land. Then he proceeded with the measures through which he hoped to re-establish senatorial predomin-ance on a firmer legal basis and to prevent constitutional attack upon it in the sphere of government; for he aimed also at setting the administration of Roman Italy in order.

The Senate needed to be much larger—perhaps twice as large—and more representative, if the body and its members were to fulfil the duties Sulla proposed to give them. He in-creased their numbers and included men from the 'equestrian' class, mostly—we may assume, since he was so hostile to the Roman *publicani*—from the landed gentry; then he provided for the entry of all ex-quaestors, now to be annually twenty in number, who had gained their administrative office by popular election. The censors thus lost their discretionary powers. This policy also supported his case for handing back the juries of the law-courts to senatorial membership, as he planned to extend their functions. At the same time, since the magistrates kept their constitutional powers in handling public business, the Senate needed defending against independent use of the consular *imperium*: the magistrates must be conditioned to the senatorial regime. Sulla redrafted the Lex Villia Annalis of 180 BC so as to enforce the order and intervals of advance-ment in office (the *cursus honorum*): praetors should normally be at least thirty-nine and consuls forty-two years of age; and no one should be re-elected to the same office—in particular, the consulship—within ten years. The consuls with eight praetors could handle administration at home and proceed, as pro-consuls or propraetors, to the governorship of the provinces, for a year; the Senate would make the appointments. Sulla extended the law of treason so as to forestall any irregular moves from a province, not least a march against Rome like his own. So much for the procedure of government—but what of popular agitation? It was tribunes who had most successfully attacked the Senate's prerogatives, and the Gracchi and Saturninus had exploited the precedents for tribunician leadership of the people. Sulla turned their case aggressively against the tribunate: let the tribunes resume their ancient function of protecting the people where the state failed to do so, and not aim at directing Roman policy. He abolished their right to introduce legislation independently and to exercise judicial powers (his law-courts covered most offences), and he limited their veto; then, by pressing tradition, since the tribunes had originally been ple-beian officers, not magistrates of the state, he made the tribunate a bar to further office.

Thus far the senatorial strategist—but Sulla was also one of the great Roman administrators. What of municipal develop-ment and the problems of law and order in Roman Italy? From this time, as the Italian cities adapted their local government to municipal status with Roman citizenship, we may trace the growth of general uniformity under boards of four magistrates (*Quattuorviri*). In criminal jurisdiction there was already a trend towards establishing permanent courts to deal with specific offences. Sulla organized this method of trial as a system to cover the major crimes: treason, extortion, peculation, electoral bribery, forgery, murder, assault; he drew the juries from the Senate. Despite the rise of legal studies in the late second cen-tury BC—we know of distinguished jurists—this development was chiefly administrative, and it would continue into the Empire.

Sulla's legislation has special interest for the student of the Late Republic, not only under historical judgement but in terms of evidence for the period. Clear-headed and ruthless he formulated measures to meet the problems of Roman government as he saw them. Our survey indicates how closely he followed a definition of the issues. It serves—in some degree—as a control on our analysis of the preceding trends; it also sharpens our perception of subsequent events. Sulla aimed at restoring in more legal form the senatorial regime of the previous century, adapted to repel the popular challenge that had emerged in the intervening years. Yet the magistrates could still go to the people, if they had the will and strength to do so, and the tribunes might well reclaim a broader initiative for their office. He had, indeed, only legislated for regular government, in the hope that the Senate would prevent further crises of policy or, if there were need for special commands, at least keep the situation under political control. He did not establish a Roman 'constitution' in the strict sense of the word. Sulla knew only too well that the ultimate sanction lay not in constitutionalism but in power. Under his policy the nobles were to exercise power through the Senate and magistracies. He had enjoyed the strong alliance of the Metelli and their political group of families, and he looked to them to provide aristocratic leadership: they expected, in effect, to succeed him; so he duly abdicated when he had reconstructed their procedure. It was the Roman nobility, not any so-called 'Sullan constitution', that faced the test of events.

The nobles were not a single-minded group. Within their aristocratic code they had their rivalries and they must have reacted variously to the aspects of Sulla's policy. Some probably found it too broad to suit their interests, others considered it too narrow in its treatment of magistrates and tribunes, while

men like Pompey kept their independence with regional support. Italy was suffering the effects of the civil war between
Sulla and the 'Marians', still divided in its loyalties at many
points: Sulla's measures of repression along with his settlement
of veterans increased local resentment and distress. It appears in
Rome itself as well as throughout Italy that economic conditions were disturbed. Clever men like Crassus might make
money, others like Catiline's associates later would try and fail,
and steady citizens in town or country were likely to lose their
security; the large estates with their gang slavery were a danger
to public order, if a Spartacus should arise. The situation was
socially unstable: politically it was unpredictable, since it
fostered boldness or desperation. A soldier, administrator and
politician of the old school, for all his keen analysis, Sulla
neglected the radical problems of Roman society, which now
involved all Italy—or, if he recognized them, he could envisage
no policy beyond the methods of harsh control. Had the nobles
learnt nothing and forgotten nothing in the growth of Roman
Italy and its overseas empire? How would they handle Sertorius, a great 'Marian' soldier in Spain? Or the pirates infesting
the Mediterranean? Or Mithridates, if he should revive his
ambitions? Then, if they had to allow special commands, how
would they impose discipline upon powerful generals? Sulla
left the nobles to meet problems which he knew he could not
solve for them. If they should fail, his dictatorship provided a
model for autocratic government—and it would only be a
matter of time before Caesar drew the logical conclusion.

Under Sulla, then, the political traditions took on legal style,
but policy still looked to personal talent. 'Traditions and men':
Ennius could define the aristocratic regime in its Roman heyday, while Cicero might lament the decline of public morality
later in a wider Italian perspective. We should not apply the
formula loosely to the Sullan age. Rome's traditions were not
sacrosanct, at least in the conventions which the oligarchy had

exploited, nor indeed in Sulla's legislation. There were able men ready to adjust them, in their essential value, to the move[,]ment of social conditions. The period we have been studying threw up strong personalities—such men as the Gracchi, Marius and Saturninus, Drusus and Sulpicius Rufus, not to forget Sulla himself and the leading nobles—all of whom played their various parts against the traditional background. This was a time of radical disruption, not of degeneracy. It roused individual thought, not inhibited by caution, and Greek literary influence improved the technique of controversy. Where tradition is challenged and defended one finds an appeal to history and, inevitably, the reinterpretation of history. The Roman records thus underwent literary elaboration, sometimes politically tendentious, often anachronistic in emphasis, and above all designed to be plausible. Much of our evidence for earlier Roman history, as we have it in Livy, is coloured by the work of the Sullan writers. Great men now justified their policy in memoirs—the material for future historians, a guide to biography—and Sulla led the fashion; we know it, in its military form, from Caesar's *Commentarii*. Perhaps the best introduction to the Late Republic is Plutarch's *Lives*. Indivi[,]dualism also found scope in the whole field of literary expres[,]sion, poetry as well as prose, as the Romans followed the Greeks into the cosmopolitan experience of the Hellenistic world. The evidence is fragmentary, because Cicero and his contemporaries would supplant their predecessors; but we should not forget them.

By the first century BC Roman art shows more confident treatment of its composite elements, whether against the Italian background or under Hellenistic influence, or by strong fusion of the two. We have contrasted the severe frieze of 'Domitius *Plates 8–12* Ahenobarbus' with a Sullan triumphal monument in Greek style, and after a stern 'veristic' portrait we have seen a similar *Plates 5, 13* kind of head set on a heroic Hellenistic body. The artistic trend reflects the cultural development of the period. Noble families and leading men celebrated their position through sculpture and on the coinage, the coins often reproducing the sculpture. Greek influence on artistic technique was no new thing, but Sulla's campaigns in the East had brought a fresh wave of Hellenism to Rome; we have to think not only of Greek models but of the actual presence of Greek craftsmen in the city. In personal terms, too, Roman individualism itself now called for expression. Whatever part the death-masks ever played in Roman art, the Romans for a century had preferred to leave a more vivid memory of themselves to posterity. The realism of contemporary Greek art served their aims, sharpened by their ruthless fidelity to their own character, in their 'veristic' por-traits. In historical terms, then, it is time to stop using 'Roman' and 'Greek' as if they were separate labels—except for the detailed analysis of technique. In art as in culture generally Rome was now Roman Italy, closely connected with the Aegean world, and the city had become a Mediterranean capi-tal. Cosmopolitan Rome was absorbing what it borrowed, as it moved through the Late Republic to its Augustan maturity.

Plates 74, 75
Plate 76

Plate 77a–c

Plate 77d–f

Plate 77g, h

I show an interesting head in the style of Caesar's portraiture and, by contrast, part of a gladiatorial scene. The coins are historically illustrative: we have noted the proud Metellan elephants and Sulla's face in profile, along with the coin of his opponent Fimbria in the East; it is a pity that we can no longer claim to see Marius and Sulla at Munich in two famous sculpted heads of the period. Roman symbolism appears in depiction of Venus on a coin celebrating Sulla, and 'Libertas' along with 'Roma' and Venus combine future hopes with an idealized ancestry. But we need not stay in Italy. I turn to Gaul after Caesar's conquest: 'Gallia' with her long dis-hevelled hair, and a Gaul, perhaps Vercingetorix himself; for here at length as well as in Italy Rome would find the true heirs of her old tradition.

CHAPTER X

Rome and the Mediterranean

OVERSEAS in the provinces, not only in Italy, we have to lift Rome's shadow from the view of regional conditions and study more freely the problems of Republican government. It is never enough to sit with an administrator: one must travel with him on circuit—with Cicero, for instance, in Cilicia—and gather the daily local impressions. Especially under indirect control, as Rome used it in local areas, the initial situation may change radically: safer communications alone will affect economic activity or require more administrative coordination; yet the very routine of colonial government may hamper measures of reform. Rome had imposed order upon Italy under loose confederate conditions but failed to meet the problems that arose with growing unification. It was much the same in the provinces, where she began by recognizing local rights and support. Her policy usually opened as what we may call 'occupation policy' in order to secure and administer a territory, making the most of the existing arrangements. That was practical procedure at the outset, especially during the course of piecemeal annexation, but it became inadequate in the long run, when it extended beyond separate provinces to involve a large part of the Mediterranean. Let us defer the charges of misgovernment, until we have examined the circumstances in which the Roman governors carried out their duties.

PROVINCIAL GOVERNMENT

The official formula is simply stated. On the annexation of territory the Roman commander and a senatorial commission of ten drew up a provincial charter, the Lex Provinciae. It dealt with administrative organization, taxation, judicial procedure,

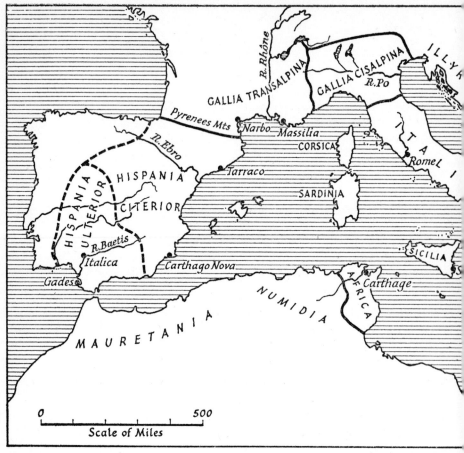

Fig. 20. Map of the Roman provinces

and local government, adapting wherever possible the previous methods in the territory. The governor could add to the regula-tions by edict, building upon precedent, so as to develop a standard system of government. Local communities, especially the cities or strong tribes, might enjoy varying degrees of autonomy: a few under treaty, others by special grant, and most

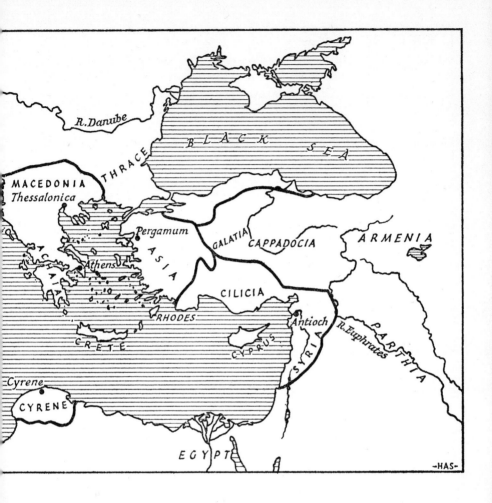

of these were exempt from taxation, while even the tribute-paying places had their local rights. The governor held over-riding powers for defence and the maintenance of general law and order, and he could claim hospitality for himself and his staff as well as the billeting of his troops. Only Roman citizens in the province had a right of appeal against his authority.

This is an administrative statement, from the Roman point of view, and it is marked by the extent of the governor's 'reserve powers'. Historically it leaves open a number of urgent ques, tions. The provinces differed in social character and they were annexed during a long period, in which Rome herself was changing. What happened meantime that might give rise to future difficulties? The governors had wide discretion. How well did they use it under the regional conditions? If they ruled badly, how effectively could they be controlled? Local privi, leges implied some moral obligation in return. What might a governor expect, how would a city anticipate his demands, and how might he exploit this situation? One could offer profit, able honours as an easy form of political bribery—the Hellenis, tic cities were used to it—and even moderate governors might be susceptible; among the unscrupulous it encouraged blatant extortion. Once the Roman *publicani* expanded their financial operations, how would they affect economic conditions, especi, ally in the East? And as enterprising Italians emigrated, how welcome would they be in the provinces? To ask these ques, tions is to show, in social terms, that the official formula is not enough. We have to study, however briefly, the historical con, ditions of Rome's provincial policy.

After the First Punic War, when Rome annexed Sicily along with Sardinia and Corsica, she aimed merely at extending Italy in order to enclose her western waters, but she had to hold the islands separately against Carthaginian recovery. The policy? It was to occupy the territory for defence, police it for internal security, and supervise the local government of the civilian population as simply as possible. Sardinia and Corsica needed only defence and policing; Sicily and its old Greek cities, already in close association with Southern Italy, called for more complex arrangements. Friends should be encouraged by favourable conditions, enemies more strictly limited. In Italy Rome had exercised this policy through treaties, and we find some treaties initially in Sicily. But, since the island was ruled by a governor, the Senate preferred to grant local autonomy, and its privileges, by declaration under his over-riding authority; it recognized the kingdom of Syracuse, and adopted its taxation system. Syracuse paid the penalty for revolt in a reorganization of the province during the Second Punic War. Sicily prospered by developing large-scale agriculture for the Roman market, while its methods of gang slavery threatened its internal order. After a great slave rising P. Rutilius in 132 BC redrafted the charter and regulations, generally following the old principles, and Cicero's *Verrines* indicates the background of administration and social life against which Verres practised his extortion in 73–71 BC. Sicily, then, provided a model for the settlement of other provinces? So it is said—in broad terms, but so broadly that the effect may mislead history. The Roman Empire was no orderly growth, even though the Romans imposed order in the end. Our brief report on Sicily is sufficient evidence: a tidy island near Italy, settled on a basis of policy but complicated in its internal relations, disturbed by external events, and dominated by Roman power, which the governors were in a position to use or abuse. Let us turn to Spain for a stronger view of the process.

The Second Punic War left Spain in Rome's hands, so far as she was able to take control. Scipio Africanus had used diplomacy as well as arms to destroy the Carthaginian power there, by alliances negotiated in the field. The problem was now to turn wartime arrangements into a more regular settlement of the country. But it was a difficult country, geographically, to bring under control. In the coastal region there were cities, Greek in the north-east, Phoenician in the south, which were ready to handle local government; inland the fierce tribes would uphold their independence, at the best in limited alliance. The situation called for military power but also a greater respect for their allies than the Romans were accustomed to concede. In 197 BC Rome defined two provinces, roughly dividing the territory between north-east and south: the cities enjoyed autonomous rights, by earlier treaty or provincial agreement, and Cato in 195 BC organized the administration and economic development. In 180–178 BC Sempronius Gracchus imposed friendly alliance upon the central tribes, largely as a personal achievement. Here was a system in principle, but it needed men to preserve it. The Spanish Wars, as we have seen, shook Rome's military strength and weakened the Senate's authority. Scipio Aemilianus restored Roman control in Spain, but his successors had to fight desperately to hold it, under conditions that must have seemed oppressive to the cities. When the 'Marian' Sertorius used his personal influence to defend Spain against Sulla's government, he could call upon Spanish nationalism: so far was the situation from provincial order; and only Pompey was able to establish a firm provincial settlement.

Fig. 20

In Greece, the Aegean, and Western Asia Minor Rome found the systematic administration of the Hellenistic states in all its variety: locally under the autonomous cities, regionally in federal relations or under the monarchies; only inland farther east the existing methods might be inadequate. There was little difficulty in extending influence, with the aid of pro-Roman parties, or in imposing provincial government by force. It was not so easy to maintain satisfactory conditions, especially if the administration ignored the social and economic problems which the very presence of external power might intensify. The process in the East was gradual and insidious. Rome had intervened against Macedon and Syria with an appeal to the old principle of Greek autonomy, and she applied a patron's influence to dominate what she had left formally independent. We have followed the painful rise of Roman imperialism: it would take fifty years to establish provincial government. In 167 BC the Macedonian kingdom was divided into four

republics and then, after Andriscus' uprising, it became a province in 148 BC; though loosely administered it still provided
a base for military control of Greece. When the Achaean
League rose in arms, Rome faced a problem of settlement. It
was one thing in 146 BC to destroy Corinth, another to suppress
Greek cities that could already claim recognition of their
autonomy. Rome left Greece nominally free but under the over-
riding authority of the governor of Macedonia, that is, not
technically a province but in a provincial position, and the
governors did not hesitate to interfere. The Greeks resented
their treatment, and Mithridates would win support; but Sulla
reduced them to subservience. After the destruction of Carthage in 146 BC, too, we may note, Rome occupied her lands
but allowed autonomous rights to the main cities in what
would be the province of 'Africa'.

When Attalus III in 133 BC bequeathed the kingdom of
Pergamum to Rome, we can follow the Romans as they took
over a complete Hellenistic organization to form the province
of 'Asia'. Administratively it was simple to annex. Rome succeeded to the royal rights and adapted the Attalid system to her
purpose. The city of Pergamum received autonomous status,
while cities previously subordinate to Pergamum and the royal
domains in the countryside remained directly under Rome,
paying their dues. Autonomous cities still kept their place; the
outlying dependencies, already practically free, were left under
their local rule. Here is the whole range of adaptable settlement.
But there were new factors. The governor exercised his over-
riding authority more strongly, for he had to watch the general
situation in Western Asia Minor; the people would feel the
weight of external power. In 132–130 BC an uprising led by
Aristonicus and the Roman measures of suppression had disturbed economic life. The province needed to recover its
balance before it contributed to the wealth of Rome. Why, then,
at this time did Tiberius Gracchus make a claim on its revenue

to further his Italian policy? And how could Gaius Gracchus farm out the collection of its taxes to the Roman *publicani*, regardless of the local effect? Honourable men, but Romans— and others would follow them in more personal exploitation. Meanwhile enterprising Italians moved in to share this busy market of the Aegean: they were too successful to be popular. 'Asia' would join Mithridates, and he ordered the massacre of eighty thousand Italians in the province. One need hardly point the moral that administrative skill alone does not constitute an imperial policy.

At this point let us examine the charges of Roman misgovernment. Administratively the procedure was correct, so far as this means anything when it leaves a large field of discretionary action. Was the tenure of office too short for governors to gain experience? It was quite long enough to allow good men to improve conditions and bad men to pursue every line of extortion. In fact, no Roman governor struggled singlehanded with his duties. He could have experienced men on his personal staff and he took over a regular team of local officials, well trained in the regulations of the province. Nor were governors slow to pass on their impressions of provincial life. The routine, then, was orderly: the fault lay higher, in lack of central control over the personal conduct of administration. The rapid turn-over of governors, if there should be more bad men than good ones, not only broke any continuity of policy but established a convention of oppressive rule. Once Augustus applied a stricter control, he could build upon the work of the Republic. Yet the situation did not depend entirely upon the governors' morality. The very flexibility of provincial arrangements, under the governor's authority, left scope for malpractice on all sides. Autonomous cities might feel an obligation to honour the representative of Rome, especially if this suited their interests. No governor would depart the poorer for his term of office. What of the duty to provide hospitality and billet troops?

A community might well take steps to win favour or buy exemption from this hardship. It was possible to compound in cash for various kinds of requisitions: Greek cities had long experience in protecting themselves by payment in the right quarter. But no one could foresee the predatory power of the Roman nobles. Let us add the increasing influence of Roman finance in the provinces. Its operations, directed as they were from Rome, took little account of local distress. The money-lenders moved in, and the more uncertain the conditions, the higher their interest; but they might reduce the risks by gaining the support of the provincial governor. Cicero was embarrassed by Brutus' loans in Cyprus—Brutus, a man (it has been said) of high principle but even higher interest! Not all governors were as blatant as Verres, but not many as scrupulous as Cicero, and few could resist the temptations of the provinces.

POMPEY

Why did Rome not develop a general policy in the Mediter-ranean as she expanded her provincial government? The Romans were slow, as they had been in Italy, to realize how their regional arrangements led to wider unification. No appeal from the provinces could move them—but the pressure of events arising from their neglect, as it had done in the Social War, drove them to action. Emergency action, and the price they would pay included the rise of powerful and ambitious men! Sertorius led Spain in a major challenge to Rome, and Pompey—against the Sullan conventions—held command from 77 till 71 BC; but the crisis was limited to the far West. When Pompey returned to Italy to help Crassus crush the uprising of Spartacus, this showed how danger could threaten Rome itself. There were wider problems, such as the spread of piracy throughout the Mediterranean. Ancient piracy reflected economic conditions and the state of politics. The Hellenistic states had policed the seas: Rome curtailed their power but failed to take over their useful functions; so piracy increased, not only from Asia Minor but around Sicily, to the point where it hampered normal communications. This was a practical problem the Romans could understand, but it called for special measures. Pirates are above all mobile and they live off their takings: they need suppressing throughout the whole area in which they sail. Early in the first century BC Rome set about reducing piracy: she established the province of Cilicia to control their bases in Asia Minor, and also occupied Cyrene and Crete. When regional action proved inadequate, she enlarged the scope of her strategy. In 67 BC Pompey received a command that covered the whole Mediterranean, with authority equal to that of provincial governors for fifty miles inland, and by coordinated operations he cleared the seas. Meanwhile Mithridates from Pontus and Tigranes of Armenia had joined in a fresh attack on Rome's position in the East. The Third Mithridatic War (74–63 BC) spread far beyond the provincial frontiers. Lucullus did most of the fighting, but in 66 BC Pompey superseded him to win the victory and make a general settlement of the East. One can hardly demand that these far-reaching events should have promoted reorganization in the actual conduct of provincial affairs: there were too many military questions, and then Rome was distracted by civil war. But the circumstances did by force bring the Eastern provinces closer together, in a wider regional association. Antony would have to go over Pompey's work; finally, when Augustus had swept the political storms away, Roman government could move towards the social and economic unification of the Mediterranean.

CHAPTER XI

From Republic to Principate

WE HAVE TRIED, as severely as Cicero or Sallust, to show how Rome struggled with her expanding problems of administration, citizenship and provincial government in their social and material setting; which may give shape to an essay on Republican Rome. We have also followed, so far, her inability to reconcile the internal differences in politics. It is time to drop the convenient label of 'Rome' and write of 'the Romans', so as to reflect the rival ambitions of men and factions that dominated the Late Republic until Augustus, the last warlord, held the field and established the Principate. Cicero might blame his contemporaries for betraying the traditions: he expressed a sound Italian attitude, with an eye to the future of responsible politics. Sallust would attack the nobles for their exclusive oligarchy, censure popular leaders like Catiline for their political irresponsibility, and lament the decline of public morality that made such things possible: he accepted the actual state of affairs. We may add that Rome's constitutional arrangements made compromise difficult, even if the traditional militarism of her politicians had not always tempted an appeal to force. Yet, when this is said, we are now dealing with men who seized the traditions and compelled them to support their personal policies. Republican Rome closes with a drama composed in human terms, against the background of a harsh social setting. Let us introduce the main characters and illustrate them from the contemporary art, in sculpture and on the coinage.

First the hard core of the oligarchic faction, which Sulla had left in control: for the most part faceless men, but none the less formidable in their determination to outlast the rise and fall of popular leaders. Perhaps the elephants of the Metelli should

Plate 77a

still represent them, drawing the chariot of Roman Jupiter! But the nobles had their spokesman, M. Porcius Cato the younger, firm in traditional doctrine, a highly skilled politician, well connected and not dangerously ambitious for himself. He would present their case, often taking it too far, and support it scrupulously until he died a symbol of the old Republic; I

Plate 78

show a recently discovered portrait, clear and intelligent in its lines. Then they had the help of Cicero, for wider reasons than they could appreciate. A good Italian, M. Tullius Cicero saw the need for Rome to draw upon the resources of talent that were now available in Roman Italy—as exemplified in himself! Why should the senatorial and equestrian classes not combine to carry Rome's responsibilities? As consul he led them against the insurgent Catiline, and later against the First Triumvirate he would restate the principle in broader terms of Italian unity. He failed, because the struggle for power in Rome exceeded his ability to control or moderate; but Augustus would take up his policy, once he was in a position to do so. We should not forget, too, that Cicero's literary genius would do more to display Roman civilization to posterity than he or his contem-poraries could ever have imagined. I show a somewhat idealiz-

Plate 79

ing portrait that yet does his character more justice, perhaps, than any 'veristic' treatment; Londoners may confirm that it represents him by studying the battered head in Apsley House.

We must revert to the stern conditions of Roman politics, where military prestige and the support of veterans—under 'military clientship'—carried more weight than the finest rhetoric, above all in the career of Pompey the Great. The war-lord Cn. Pompeius Strabo had left his son well prepared to use his own troops and regional support in maintaining an inde-pendent position. Pompey's ready power and ability made him a valuable ally at times of military crisis, even to the nobles who distrusted his ambition. He joined Sulla's side to help defeat the 'Marians' in Italy and crushed the remnants of opposition

in Sicily and Africa; then he stood by the Senate to destroy
M. Aemilius Lepidus, when the consul of 78 BC threatened its
authority by armed force. These were men with whom he had
been associated, and he did not hate them, but he executed
summary justice: the *adulescentulus carnifex* without mercy,
following the impersonal brutality of Roman militarism. For
now as at the end of his career, however insistent he was in
demanding personal glory, Pompey's traditional attitude kept
him faithful to the Republic. His was the Republic, however,
not of Sulla's routine administration but of grand strategy,
where the Senate in the past had called its outstanding men to
high command and respected their personal honour and
authority; nor was he the only leading Roman of his time to
claim this traditional privilege. Thus he took almost as a right
his appointment to command against Sertorius in Spain and
later against the pirates and Mithridates. With every success he
enlarged his political patronage, both in Italy among his
veterans and in the provinces where he imposed personal
obligations in the course of settling affairs. Hence his influence
in Rome, silent but strong. But he did not feel bound to the
restrictive measures of Sulla's policy, and as consul with Crassus in 70 BC he modified it so as to restore the freer action of
the second century BC, with the tribunes and censors exercising
their functions once again. When he joined in the First Triumvirate, this was to maintain—against oligarchic opposition—
what he regarded as his due authority in the Republic; nor did
he fail, if we think of his supreme position as sole consul and
proconsular governor of Spain in 52 BC. There was no disgrace,
on his own terms, in falling before a greater man of the same
tradition, Julius Caesar.

How could an artist depict Pompey? His waving hair and
smooth facial contours, especially in a portrait executed with
Hellenistic grace, need not betray his inner hardness. We may
think we know Pompey from the Ny Carlsberg head: it may

Plate 80
Plate 81a-d

well be a true Imperial copy of its Republican original, but any impression of weakness is illusory; I prefer to show a less stylized contemporary portrait. Pompey's sons celebrated their father on their coins, as they upheld his cause: Pompey's face in profile, Pompey riding in triumph, and Pompey with his sons, carrying on his Republican tradition.

We have studied the social changes in Italy during the second century BC, which set the pattern of the Late Republic. It is important now to stress two fresh factors, one over-stimulating, the other depressing, in the years after the Social War and the fighting between Sulla and the 'Marians', when the country needed to consolidate its political organization and regain economic stability. First, the equestrian *publicani* strengthened their position and expanded their activities, especially in the East after the First Mithridatic War, by lending money profit-ably to the cities which had to pay the arrears of taxes and severe indemnities. In Rome, too, they increased their financial enterprise and exercised more pressure in politics, not so much to make policy as to secure their interests under whatever policy was put forward. Secondly, the social aftermath of civil war, marked by the cruel 'proscriptions' and confiscation of property and in rural areas by the settlement of veterans, had disturbed the normal course of life and work in Rome and Central Italy. Powerful financiers and wealthy landowners could face the difficulties and even benefit from them: smaller businessmen and the poorer landed gentry lost their security and confidence and were slow to recover. We find reference to the problem of 'indebtedness'. Did some debasement of the coinage—by pass-ing silver-plated coins of bronze or copper as *denarii*, with or without the connivance of the state—ease the situation, until Sulla legislated against the practice? We learn that it caused popular panic about 86 BC; but we may not argue about in-flationary trends in the Roman economy at this time. The problem of financial distress would remain to encourage any

radical politician in a call for 'cancellation of debts'. But enterprising men exploited the opportunity, not only the *publicani* but
the senators, since a public career required the popular use of
wealth. Politicians incurred debt as a personal investment, for
which the provinces might ultimately pay: if they failed, they
would join the radical malcontents; if they succeeded, there was
no limit to their private prospects. Against this background
Crassus made money and bought political influence, Catiline
failed, and Julius Caesar used the means to achieve his political
ambitions.

M. Licinius Crassus joined Sulla to distinguish himself as a
soldier and gain influence in senatorial circles, without com-
mitting his loyalty to the dictator's regime. His business flair,
well adapted to the awkward times, especially for speculation
in property, earned him a fortune and made him a leader in
Roman finance: he was as close to the *publicani* as to the Senate,
while he pursued a political career. His command against
Spartacus increased his military standing and authority in
Italian affairs. Then as consul with Pompey in 70 BC he
restored the pre-Sullan flexibility of Roman politics that suited
the wide scope of the interests he represented. His wealth and
enterprise enabled him to support—profitably—many promis-
ing politicians in their various aims, and he exercised a per-
vasive influence, often indirectly, alongside the rigid policy of
Cato and the nobles on the one hand and Pompey's great
Eastern commands on the other. A subtle man and successful,
until he left himself open to a Parthian shot! By contrast L.
Sergius Catilina, able but violently ambitious, illustrates under
the same conditions how one might provoke general resistance
by threatening too many rival interests at the one time. He, too,
had risen as a lieutenant of Sulla and done well out of the dis-
orders; but he fell back in the running for the consulship and
determined to press a radical programme, including a cancellation of debts, in order to play on the discontent that was still

bitterly felt in many parts of Italy. Failing again he turned to armed insurrection, and it was Cicero as consul in 63 BC who crushed him, with senatorial and equestrian support. Sallust uses the episode to illustrate the degeneration of Roman life: it certainly shows the political and social difficulties that con⁄ tinued to afflict the Late Republic.

CAESAR

Amid the opportunities and dangers of the time Julius Caesar plotted a general course—no more—along which to direct his political ambition. Historical sentiment had now begun to serve the aims of policy: the nobles paraded their ancestry even on the coinage, and the appeal had shifted still further back to the regal age and the Trojan foundation of Rome. Sulla a 'Romulus' come to judgement, for better or worse? Or had Venus forgotten her descendants? No family could boast a higher antiquity than the Julii, as they looked beyond the Alban kings to Iulus, Aeneas, and Venus Genetrix herself: Caesar was the pure patrician aristocrat, in temperament as well as pride, and he would die for his style. But at this point, as he well knew, a warlord father was worth more than Mars and Venus together! Pompey could move from strength, Caesar had to gain his position. He survived his 'Marian' connections without denying them, and then he followed a regular public career: military service in the East, legal practice in Rome, and the normal offices, until he became praetor in 62 BC and went out as governor to Farther Spain. This experience was as valuable for him as it had been for Crassus; and, as Crassus developed his financial interests, so Caesar for his part set out to impress popular opinion. He realized, as Pompey had not learnt, that political finesse was necessary to the use of power within Rome itself, and he prepared the ground while he waited for the command that would establish him. Spectacular

public entertainment combined with the pursuit of priestly
office brought the image of a true 'Julian' up to date, and he
was elected to the highest religious place in the state as Pontifex
Maximus. When he needed to borrow money, such men as
Crassus considered him a good risk. In politics Caesar ranked
among the Populares, often in association with Crassus: in
other words, he wanted a freer hand than the strict senatorial
procedure of the Optimates would allow. For instance, he
joined in the popular approval of Pompey's Eastern commands
and opposed Cicero's summary execution of Catiline's supporters in Rome. In any problem foreshadowing the kind of
situation in which he might find himself involved later, he was
determined to limit the scope of dangerous precedents of policy.
We need not believe that Caesar aimed from the outset at
establishing an autocracy: in the ancient evidence as well as in
modern views this is to argue after the event; but he fixed his
keen eye on the political path towards dominant power in the
Republic. The consular *imperium*, firmly exercised with popular
support, and a great military command to continue it, would
secure his honour and authority; then he could meet the unpredictable emergencies. This was Caesar's method in politics as
in war—to engage carefully and then take his chance. There are
portraits of Caesar in the Hellenistic style which the Romans
adapted to their purpose; I show the head that illustrates most
clearly his hard intelligence and power of action; a coin in
'veristic' style gives his profile. When he fell under Brutus'
daggers of the Ides of March in 44 BC, he left Rome to conjure
with the Julian name.

Plate 83

Plate 82a

Plate 82b, c

We have called up personalities not only for their influence
in the Republic but to illustrate the new complexity of Roman
politics. The importance of overseas commands, the growth of
financial enterprise, and the move towards wider political
action combine to show how government and administration
had to operate on an imperial scale. The problems that had

emerged in the second century BC to demand special treatment were now part of general policy. Where Sulla legislated for normal procedure, the limits of normalcy had expanded: circumstances as well as the amendments to his work changed the situation. Yet the nobles still held their old ground, aided by the political skill of Cato, rejecting Cicero's appeal for cooperation between the senatorial and equestrian orders. They thought in terms of a struggle for power in Rome, where they might exploit the Senate's prerogatives. The issues, in fact, brought stronger forces into play, if they could be focused politically on the Roman scene. By 60 BC Pompey expected ratification of his Eastern settlement and the provision of land for his veterans, Crassus was supporting the *publicani* for a rebate on their contract for the collection of taxes, and Caesar wanted to celebrate a triumph from Spain and stand for the consulship. These were matters that required liberal consideration, not the obstruction of narrow politics. Cato blocked them all. Then the storm broke over the Roman Forum. Pompey, Crassus and Caesar joined in the so-called 'First Triumvirate'. The label is an informal one: it simply indicates a political alliance such as the nobles had among themselves, but covering a wider field of operations; its purpose was to gain immediate satisfaction for the individual demands of the three men and prevent further oligarchic obstruction in the future. Their cooperation did not exclude independent action, within the bounds of compatibility. The Triumvirate had its way. Caesar as consul of 59 BC carried the necessary legislation and then proceeded to a five years' provincial command in Gaul; thus he got his hands at last on military power.

What were the political mechanics of this over-riding move? Constitutional arrangements in Rome allowed little compromise, and popular legislation was usually accompanied by violence. The Triumvirate concentrated their prestige and authority, generous bribery, and the use of organized violence from the outset to check all opposition. Cato was sent to annex Cyprus, Cicero was exiled (58–57 BC), and such agitators as Clodius and Milo had free play. Of course there was opposition. Cicero extended his policy of combining the senatorial and equestrian orders to the Italian bourgeoisie as a whole: his difficulty was to apply it directly to the political situation by Optimate procedure; meanwhile the nobles held their ground and watched for a rift in the Triumvirate. The Triumvirate renewed their alliance at Luca in 56 BC, and Pompey and Crassus took their second joint consulship the next year: Caesar received a five years' extension in Gaul, Pompey the governorship of Spain (to be exercised from Rome through legates), and Crassus a command in Syria against the Parthians. Here we see the essential factor—to rule the empire and bring power to bear on Rome itself. But whose power? The three men were still pursuing their individual ambitions. The Parthians removed Crassus at Carrhae in 53 BC. Disorder in Rome raised Pompey to the height of his authority in 52 BC as sole consul and still governor of Spain. Caesar conquered Gaul and looked forward to a second consulship, which should lead to another great command, presumably in the East. Now at last the issue of power arose between Pompey and Caesar, on equal terms, and the nobles won Pompey to the traditional side; then they precipitated the Civil War (49–45 BC). The better soldier won, and it was Caesar, not Pompey, who became dictator of Rome, prepared to develop Sulla's position.

From 49 till 45 BC, holding variously the dictatorship or consulship, Caesar exercised supreme power to face the emergencies of civil war. How long then would he need to make a peaceful settlement? In early February 44 BC he took the dictatorship for life, with such regal honours as a Julian succeeding Sulla might well assume. He would be king? Whatever the title, his term of rule could only be ended by death: the nobles cut it short on the Ides of March. I show the head of Brutus,   Plate 82b, c

169

Fig. 21. Ides of March

(*a*) *Denarius* (c. *44 BC; L. Aemilius Buca*). *Head of Caesar,* PERPETVO CAESAR DICT.
(*b*) *Denarius* (*43–42 BC*). *Head of Brutus, L. PLAET. CEST. BRVT. IMP.; cap of liberty
between two daggers, EID. MAR.* (Eidibus Martiis)

Fig. 21   the daggers, and the cap of liberty on the Republicans' coinage.
But they had not kept up with the times. A dictator set above
the constitution: let him be removed, and normal government
will return? The standards of normalcy in administration and
politics had shifted far beyond their conception of the Republic.
Caesar's legislation, like that of Sulla, indicates the situation as
he saw it. Here we need not enter into the details: it is the coordination of measures that is significant. In practical ways he
aimed at making Rome a capital worthy of its imperial position, and he drafted regulations to assist the municipal development of Italy, already far advanced, so as to unify the country.
He eased the distinction between Italy and the provinces,
especially as he planned overseas settlement for his veterans and
needy citizens; he extended Latin status as a step towards
citizenship; and he did not hesitate to draw provincials into
Roman life, even in the Senate. This was historical logic, formulated by a statesman who accepted the implications of
Rome's success.

Caesar's death revived the issue of power, while Italy and
the provinces waited for the general settlement which Rome
owed to the Mediterranean. Brutus and his supporters—and

Cicero, too, emerging briefly as leader of the Republic—under/estimated the strength of Antony, who succeeded to Caesar's armed power; and not only they but Antony also took Octa/vian too lightly, the dictator's grand/nephew and adoptive son, who inherited his military patronage and political influence as well as the appeal of the Julian name. We need not follow the details of civil war. In 43 BC Antony, Octavian and M. Aemi/lius Lepidus joined in the Second Triumvirate, this time an official commission exercising supreme authority. By 'pro/scriptions' they crushed all opposition in Italy—thus Cicero died—and they defeated Brutus and Cassius at Philippi in 42 BC. Only Sextus Pompey remained to uphold his father's name and cause on the high seas. The Triumvirs divided the Roman world under their command, Antony taking the East, Octavian and Lepidus the West. In terms of power the issue would lie between Antony and Octavian; but we should not anticipate the clash. While Antony settled the East and planned war against Parthia, Octavian's task was to limit Sextus Pom/pey and restore stable conditions in Italy and the West. The two men combined—or, rather, Antony helped Octavian—in handling this situation, and in 40 BC Antony married Octavia, Octavian's sister, a significant act in the play of Roman politics; Virgil—in his Fourth Eclogue—would celebrate hopes of the future. With Agrippa's help Octavian defeated Sextus Pom/pey and deposed Lepidus; then he organized Italy in his own name.

Plate 82d

In the East, where Egypt afforded the best base for major military operations, Antony had met Cleopatra VII, successor to what was left of the Ptolemaic power. At the age of twenty/two she had wooed Julius Caesar from any designs on her kingdom: now at twenty/nine, the age (according to Plutarch) at which a Graeco/Macedonian woman was at her best in mind and body—and she was cultured as well as attractive—she set herself to capture Antony. I have pleasure—thanks to recent finds—in introducing both Antony and Cleopatra in contemporary portraits, along with the evidence of the coins. Antony shows his rugged features: some (we are told) thought him dignified, others like a gladiator, and perhaps both opinions were right. Cleopatra is plain but she must have been fascinating; the nose of her portrait is a neutral (modern) restoration, and coins are usually unkind to noses. A firm Macedonian queen, who needed no Oriental glamour to assist her 'infinite variety', she was a woman after the Roman's heart. Let us view the heads together—as far as faces reflect character— to feel their compatibility; for they would join in threatening the Roman tradition. Antony left Octavia to marry Cleopatra (if not in 37, then in 33 BC) and establish his position in Hellenistic style. They failed at Actium in 31 BC, and Shakespeare using the best of Plutarch's *Lives* has preserved the picture. Octavian remained alone in the field; I give an early portrait, with coins celebrating his success.

Plate 84a, b
Plate 85a, b
Plate 86
Plate 87a–c

Struggle for political power is a narrow thing, justified only by the scope it may allow for broader government and social development. The Romans of the Republic had conquered other peoples and then turned their strength inwards on the state, as it expanded in size and complexity. At home as abroad they accepted no compromise, so the issues of power were fought out to the bitter end. Yet all the time their practical genius was turning experience into method, which could be applied—in defence, administration, and provincial growth—once the political situation was settled. Octavian took control the hard Roman way, following Caesar's example, but he adapted Pompey's precedents for high command, and he accepted what Cicero had taught about the quality of Italian support. Then —let us now call him Augustus—he established the Roman peace. If it involved dynastic rule, that is another story—the history of the Roman Empire.

Select Bibliography

This essay imposes its strict pattern upon a select bibliography. First, since it treats the critical stages of Roman development, it may lack con~ tinuity of narrative: we must make this good by reference to general history. Secondly, while it adduces social, political and material evidence, it may obscure the growth of these various factors in their own context: we need to cite the special works. I list the studies that help to clarify and amplify, and enable the reader to modify, the terms of my interpretation. One need only mention the *Cambridge Ancient History*, the *Histoire Générale* (ed. Glotz), and the *Storia di Roma* (Istituto di Studi Romani), or such scholarly aids as Pauly~Wissowa's *Real~Encyclopädie*, the brilliant *Enciclo~ pedia Italiana*, and the useful *Oxford Classical Dictionary* (1949, now revising), the last well adapted to provide concise detail about institutions, personalities and events. Most modern studies are in debt to G. De Sanctis, *Storia dei Romani* (1907–). For the rest we may consider the works that are immediately relevant to the subject~matter of the essay.

General History

(Bibliographical survey: A. H. McDonald, 'Fifty Years of Republican History', *Journ. Rom. Studies*, 50 (1960), p. 135.)

ADCOCK, F. E., *Roman Political Ideas and Practice* (1959).

CARY, M., *History of Rome* (1935).

—, *Geographic Background of Greek and Roman History* (1949).

HEICHELHEIM, F. M. and YEO, C. A., *History of the Roman People* 1962).

HEUSS, A., *Römische Geschichte* (1960).

HOFMANN, A. VON, *Das Land Italien und seine Geschichte* (1921).

HOMO, L., *Roman Political Institutions* (1929).

MEYER, E., *Römischer Staat und Staatsgedanke* (rev. ed., 1961).

ROSTOVTZEFF, M., *Rome* (1928, now paperback).

SCULLARD, H. H., *History of the Roman World, 753–146 BC* (rev. ed., 1951).
—, *From the Gracchi to Nero* (1959, now paperback).
SEMPLE, E. C., *Geography of the Mediterranean Region* (1932).
TOYNBEE, A. J., *Hannibal's Legacy* (1965).

II *Historical Authorities*

(Bibliographical survey: A. H. McDonald, 'The Roman Historians', Ch. 13, *Fifty Years of Classical Scholarship*, ed. M. Platnauer, 1954.)
GIANNELLI, G., *Trattato di storia romana*, I (1953).
LEWIS, N. and REINHOLD, M., *Roman Civilization*, I (1951).
PIGANIOL, A., *Histoire de Rome* (3rd ed., 1949).
ROSENBERG, A., *Einleitung und Quellenkunde zur römischen Geschichte* (1921).
SYME, R., *Sallust* (1964).
WALSH, P. G., *Livy* (1961).

III *Italy and Rome*

ALFÖLDI, A., *Early Rome and the Latins* (1965).
BLOCH, R., *The Etruscans* (1958).
—, *The Origins of Rome* (1960).
CHILVER, G. E. F., *Cisalpine Gaul* (1941).
FRACCARO, P., 'La storia romana arcaica', *Opuscula*, I, 3 (1956), cf. *Journ. Rom. Studies*, 47 (1957), p. 59.
GJERSTAD, E., *Legends and Facts of Early Roman History* (1962).
—, *Etruscan Culture* (Swedish Inst. in Rome), 1962, p. 145: 'Etruscans and Rome in Archaic Times'.
HEURGON, J., *Capoue préromaine* (1942).
POWELL, T. G. E., *The Celts* (1958).
SHERWIN-WHITE, A. N., *The Roman Citizenship* (1939).
WERNER, R., *Der Beginn der römischen Republik* (1963).
WHATMOUGH, J., *The Foundations of Roman Italy* (1937).
WOODHEAD, A. G., *The Greeks in the West* (1962).

IV *Roman Expansion*

BADIAN, E., *Foreign Clientelae* (1958).
—, *Studies in Greek and Roman History* (1964).
COOK, J. M., *The Greeks in Ionia and the East* (1962).
FRANK, T., *Roman Imperialism* (1914).
HARDEN, D., *The Phoenicians* (1962).
MAGIE, D., *Roman Rule in Asia Minor* (1950).
ROSTOVTZEFF, M., *Social and Economic History of the Hellenistic World* (1953).
—, *Social and Economic History of the Roman Empire* (2nd ed., rev. P. M. Fraser, 1957).
SCULLARD, H. H., *Roman Politics, 220–150 BC* (1951).
SUTHERLAND, C. H. V., *The Romans in Spain* (1939).
TARN, W. W. and GRIFFITH, G. T., *Hellenistic Civilization* (3rd ed., 1952).
WALBANK, F. W., *Philip V of Macedon* (1940).
WARMINGTON, B., *Carthage* (1960).

V *Roman Society and Culture*

ALTHEIM, F., *History of Roman Religion* (1938).
BALSDON, J. P. V. D., *Roman Women* (1962).
— (ed.), *The Romans* (1965).
FINLEY, M. I. (ed.), *Slavery in Classical Antiquity* (1960).
FOWLER, W. WARDE, *Social Life in Rome in the Age of Cicero* (1908, now paperback).
—, *The Religious Experience of the Roman People* (1922).
FRANK, T., *Economic History of Rome* (1927).
—, *Life and Letters in the Roman Republic* (1930, now paperback).
—, *Economic Survey of Ancient Rome*, I, 'Republic' (1933).
GELTZER, M., *Die Nobilität der römischen Republik* (1912); now in *Kl. Schr.* I, p. 17 (1962).
GRIMAL, P., *Le siècle des Scipions* (1953).
HEITLAND, W. E., *Agricola* (1921).
KROLL, W., *Die Kultur der ciceronischen Zeit* (1933).

LATTE, K., *Römische Religionsgeschichte* (1960).
PAOLI, U. E., *Rome, its People, Life and Customs* (1963).
SMITH, R. E., *The Failure of the Roman Republic* (1955).
WEBSTER, T. B. L., *Hellenistic Poetry and Art* (1964), for early Roman literature.
WIRSZUBSKI, CH., *Libertas as a Political Idea at Rome* (1950).

VI *Roman Art*

BIEBER, M., *The Sculpture of the Hellenistic Age* (rev. ed., 1961).
ESSEN, CH./CL. VAN, *Précis d'histoire de l'art antique en Italie* (Coll. Latomus, 1960).
HANFMANN, G. M. A., *Roman Art* (1964).
PICARD, G. C., *L'art romain* (1962).
RICHTER, G. M. A., *Ancient Italy* (1955).
RYBERG, I. S., *Rites of the State Religion in Roman Art* (1955).
STRONG, E., *Art in Ancient Rome* (1929).
—, *Camb. Anc. Hist.* IX, Ch. 20; Plates Vol. IV.
TOYNBEE, J. M. C., *The Art of the Romans* (1965).
WHEELER, R. E. M., *Roman Art and Architecture* (1964).

VII *Roman Architecture and Monuments*

(See E. Nash, *Pictorial Dictionary of Ancient Rome*, 1961.)
ANDERSON, W. J., SPIERS, R. P. and ASHBY, T., *The Architecture of Ancient Rome* (1927).
ASHBY, T., *The Aqueducts of Ancient Rome* (1935).
BOETHIUS, A., *The Golden House of Nero* (1960); also for Italian town-planning.
BROWN, F. E., *Roman Architecture* (1961).
LUGLI, G., *Roma antica: il centro monumentale* (1946).
—, *La tecnica edilizia romana* (1957).
PLATNER, S. B. and ASHBY, T., *Topographical Dictionary of Ancient Rome* (1929).
ROBATHAN, D. M., *The Monuments of Ancient Rome* (1950).

ROBERTSON, D. S., *Handbook of Greek and Roman Architecture* (1954).

ROMANELLI, P., *Il Palatino* (1950).

—, *The Roman Forum* (1950).

RYBERG, I. S., *Archaeological Record of Rome from 7th to 2nd cent. BC* (1940).

VITRUVIUS, trans. M. H. Morgan (1914, now paperback).

WINSLOW, E. M., *Libation to the Gods* (1963), on aqueducts.

VIII *Italian Archaeology*

BLAKE, M. P., *Ancient Roman Construction in Italy* (1947).

BRADFORD, J., *Ancient Landscapes* (1957).

CARRINGTON, R. C., *Pompeii* (1936).

FREDERIKSEN, M. W., 'Republican Capua', *Papers Brit. School at Rome*, XXVII (N.S. XIV), 1959, p. 80.

MACKENDRICK, P., *The Mute Stones Speak* (1962; note bibliography).

MEIGGS, R., *Roman Ostia* (1960).

WARD-PERKINS, J. B., 'Early Roman Towns in Italy', *Town Planning Review*, 26 (1955), p. 127.

—, 'Veii: Historical Topography of the Ancient City', *Papers Brit. School at Rome* XXIX (N.S. XVI), 1961.

WYCHERLEY, R. E., *How the Greeks built Cities* (1949).

IX *Roman Coins of the Republic*

CARSON, R. A. G. and SUTHERLAND, C. H. V. (ed.), *Roman Coinage* (1956).

MATTINGLY, H., *Roman Coins* (rev. ed., 1960).

SYDENHAM, E. A., *The Roman Republican Coinage* (1952).

THOMSEN, R., *Early Roman Coinage*, 2 vol. (1957–61).

X *The Late Republic*

COBBAN, J. M., *Senate and Provinces, 78–49 BC* (1935).

FRANK, T. (ed.), *Economic Survey of Ancient Rome*, Vol. III–IV (1937–1938), on the provinces.

HILL, H., *The Roman Middle Class* (1952).

HOLMES, T. RICE, *The Roman Republic* (1923).

—, *The Architect of the Roman Empire*, I (1928).

JONES, A. H. M., *The Cities of the Eastern Roman Provinces* (1937).

SMITH, R. E., *Service in the Post-Marian Army* (1958).

—, *Cicero* (in the press).

STEVENSON, G. H., *Roman Provincial Administration* (1939).

SYME, R., *The Roman Revolution* (1939, now paperback).

TARN, W. W. and CHARLESWORTH, M. P., *Octavian, Antony and Cleopatra* (1965, paperback=Camb. Anc. Hist. X, Ch. 1–4).

TAYLOR, L. R., *Party Politics in the Age of Caesar* (1961).

THE PLATES

5

6

11

12

13

14

15

6

7

18

21

22

23

24

25

26

27

29

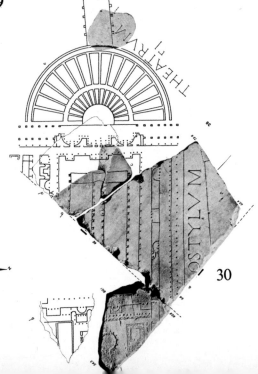

30

31

32

33

34

35

36

37

38

39

40

41

43

45

46

48

49

50

51

54

55

56

57

58

59

60

61

63

64

66

67

68

69

-70

C 71

72

73

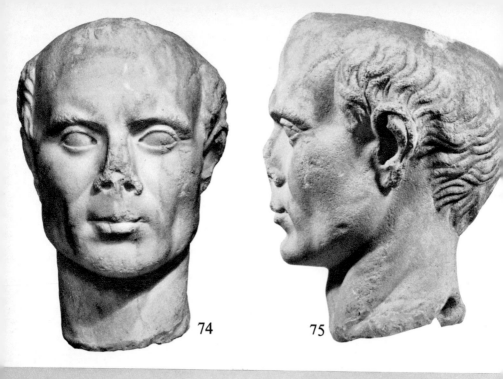

74   75

76

a

b

c

d

e

f

g

h

77

78

79

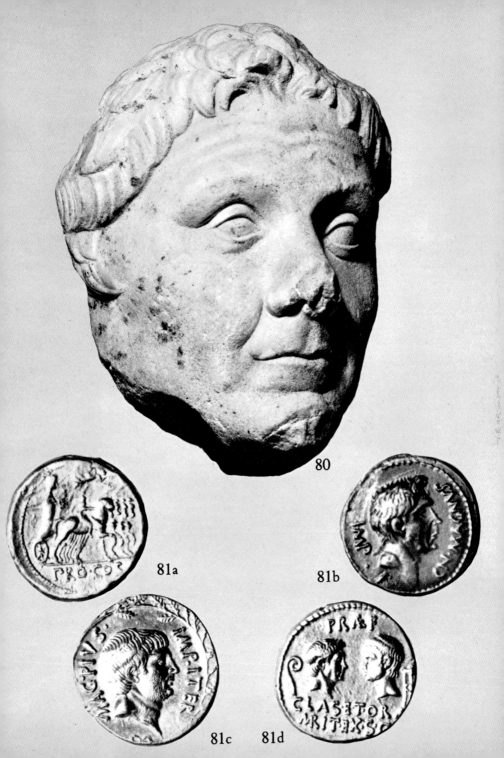

80

81a

81b

81c 81d

82 a

82 b

83

82 c

82 d

84 b

84 a

85 b

85 a

86

87 a

87 b

87

Notes on the Plates

As the plates are chosen not only to illustrate but to share equally with the text and figures in treating Republican Rome, I have discussed them fully in the text. These notes can be brief, except where they need to explain details; I give page references to the text; sometimes I cite works that are strictly relevant to the notes, e.g. Syd. = E. A. Sydenham, *Coinage of the Roman Republic* (1952). I have to thank Museums and Institutes as well as photographers for the provision of photographs and for permission to print—especially Ernest Nash ('Fot.' = Fototeca Unione). I note the Museums where monuments may be seen and (in brackets) the photographers, normally for each plate in turn; but I would acknowledge here the courtesy of J. B. Ward-Perkins for plates 20–22, P. H. Blanckenhagen and J. B. Ward-Perkins for plates 67–69, and G. D. B. Jones and the Apulia Committee of the Society of Antiquaries for plates 70–73.

1 Marble statue of patrician carrying busts of ancestors: statue late Augustan, busts copying heads of different dates of first century BC. Rome: Mus. Capit., Braccio Nuovo (Alinari 28567). See p. 90.

2, Peperine head, front and side, of so-called 'Ennius', from Tomb of
3 Scipios: early second century BC. Mus. Vat. (Arch. Fot. Vat. XXXII, 127, 11–12). See p. 91.

4 Peperine sarcophagus of L. Scipio Barbatus (consul 298 BC) from Tomb of Scipios. Inscription (early second century BC) reads: CORNELIVS LVCIVS SCIPIO BARBATVS GNAIVOD PATRE/PROGNATVS FORTIS VIR SAPIENSQVE—QVOIVS FORMA VIRTVTEI PARISVMA/FVIT CONSOL CENSOR AIDILIS QVEI FVIT APVD VOS—TAVRASIA CISAVNA/SAMNIO CEPIT SVBIGIT OMNE LOVCANVM OPSIDESQVE ABDOVCIT. Mus. Vat. (Fot. 10560). See p. 91.

5 Veiled head of old Roman (sacrificing?): first century BC. Mus. Vat. (Alinari 27020). See p. 91.

6 Bronze head of so-called 'Brutus': presumably Etrusco-Roman of late fourth century BC. But difficult to date: perhaps third century BC—and, as an idealized portrait, even of first century BC; also even suspected as a Renaissance work. Rome: Pal. Conservatori (Alinari 6030). See p. 91.

7 Coins of third century BC (didrachms), except g, h (denarii). *Cf.* R. Thomsen, *Early Roman Coinage*, I, Ch. 2; II, p. 356.
   (a, b) Hercules (obv.); wolf and twins, *ROMANO* (rev.). London: Brit. Mus. (Syd. 6, *c.* 269 BC). See pp. 91–2.
   (c) Mars. Brit. Mus. (Syd. 1, *c.* 269 BC). See p. 92.
   (d, e) Janus (obv.); Jupiter in quadriga, *ROMA* (rev.). Cambridge: Fitzwilliam Mus. (cf. Syd. 64, *c.* 222 BC). See p. 92.
   (f) Diana. Brit. Mus. (Syd. 21, *c.* 241 BC). See p. 92.
   (g) (Denarius) Roma, *ROMA*. Fitzwilliam Mus. (cf. Syd. 543; moneyer A. Manlius, *c.* 100 BC). See p. 92.
   (h) (Early denarius) Dioscuri, *ROMA*. Brit. Mus. (Syd. 140, but rather end third century BC; anon.). See p. 92.

8, Reliefs of so-called 'Altar of Domitius Ahenobarbus' (height, 82 cm.):
9, mid-first century BC. Not army 'lustratio' (purification) or demobilization
10 of veterans, but rather 'census' of Roman People: R. M. Ogilvie, *JRS* 51 (1961), p. 37. From Rome, now in Paris, Louvre; panel of Neptune and Amphitrite: Munich, Glyptothek (Alinari 22556–8). See pp. 93–4.

11, Two panels, in grey limestone, of triumphal relief found at SE angle of
12 Capitoline hill: early first century BC, Sullan. Rome: Pal. Conservatori, Bracchio Nuovo. Sulla's victory at Chaeronea?
    11 Victories adorning with laurel a shield displaying an eagle.
    12 Decorated cuirass, trophies of armour flanking a shield with helmeted head of Roma.
    See pp. 94, 149–50; and D. E. Strong, *Roman Imperial Sculpture*, p. 12.

13 'Roman general' from Tivoli: early first century BC. Rome: Mus. Nazionale (Anderson 28853). See p. 94, 149–50.

14 Relief of Mettius Curtius: Imperial copy of Republican panel at Lacus Curtius in Roman Forum. (Cast: Fot. 10372). See p. 94.

15 Relief of knights—from alabaster urn of Volterra (height, 41 cm.): second (or first?) century BC. Not annual procession of *equites* to temple but rather funeral procession to shrine. London: Brit. Mus. See pp. 94–5.

16, Baking reliefs from Tomb of Vergilius Eurysaces: late first century BC.
17 Rome: Porta Maggiore (Alinari 6736, A, B). *Cf.* M. Rostovtzeff, *Soc. Econ. Hist. Rom. Emp.* (2nd ed.), p. 32. See p. 95.

18 Tomb of Vergilius Eurysaces at Porta Maggiore, Rome: late Republican or early Augustan. Inscription reads: (EST HOC MONVMENTVM) MARCEI VERGILEI EVRISACIS PISTORIS REDEMPTORIS APPARET. (*apparitoris*)— baker, contractor, magistrate's attendant (Fot. 5615). See p. 95.

19 Veii: Temple of 'Apollo' (Fot. 7393). See p. 100.

20 Veii: wall (photo, J.B.W./P.). *Cf.* J. B. Ward/Perkins, 'Veii', *Papers Brit. School Rome*, XXIX (N.S. XVI), 1961; also for pl. 21, 22. See p. 100.

21 Veii: NE gate (photo: J.B.W./P.). See above, pl. 20, and p. 100.

22 Veii: roads from NW gate, right to Nepi, left to Vulci and Tarquinia (photo: J.B.W./P.). See above, pl. 20, and p. 100.

23 Ostia: Imperial forum area, basilica in foreground, as site of the old 'castrum' and Republican centre (Fot. 2241); *cf.* R. Meiggs, *Roman Ostia*, Ch. 3. See pp. 100–1.

24 Ostia: wall of 'castrum' (Fot. 1917). See above, pl. 23 and p. 100.

25 Ostia: central part, air view (Fot. 6141). *Cf.* J. Bradford, *Anc. Land-scapes*, pl. 58–61, pp. 239 ff. See p. 100–1.

26 Cloaca Maxima and Forum Boarium from Tiber (Alinari 6231); river bank now with modern embankment, arched efflux for Cloaca Maxima. See p. 101.

D. E. Strong and J. B. Ward-Perkins, 'The Temple of Castor', *Papers Brit. School Rome*, XXX (N.S. XVII), 1962, p. 1. See pp. 110–1.

42   Temple of Vesta and Regia (Fot. 10896). See pp. 111–2.

43   Air view of Regia (Fot. 3217). See p. 112.

44   Forum Romanum from Capitol end (Fot. 9082). See pp. 112–6 and Fig. 16.

45   Lid-handle of bronze *cista* (coffer) from Praeneste: mid-fourth century BC; two young warriors carrying a third—'the fallen comrade'. Cambridge, Fitzwilliam Mus. See p. 118.

46   Bronze figurine of Gaul (height, 5¼ in.): late third century BC, found near Rome; note Celtic torc and belt, with horned helmet, the pose to cast a spear. Berlin, Staatl. Mus. (Ger. Arch. Inst. 40,775). *Cf.* T. G. E. Powell, *The Celts*, pl. 1. See p. 119.

47   Bronze statuette of Samnite warrior (height, 29·2 cm.): fifth century BC or later archaizing style; if found in Sicily, still of Campanian style: *cf.* M. Rostovtzeff. *Rome*, pl. 10, 1. Paris, Louvre (Ger. Arch. Inst. 38,640). See p. 119.

48   Norba: city walls and gate, fourth century BC (Alinari 20292). See p. 119.

49   Falerii: city wall and gate, third century BC (Fot. 10587). See pp. 119–20.

50   Cosa: air view of site and harbour (Fot. 4254). *Cf.* J. Bradford, *Anc. Landscapes*, pl. 54–55, pp. 227 ff. See p. 122.

51   Cosa: forum area with basilica, stage building (Fot. 2914). See p. 122.

52   Tarracina: terrace of Temple of Jupiter Anxur, late second/early first century BC (Fot. 3725). See pp. 123–4.

53   Ferentinum: barrel vault of warehouse, late second/early first century BC (Fot. 3298). See p. 124.

54   Alba Fucens: across market to basilica platform, *tabernae* below, Mt Velino in background (Fot. 3109). See p.123.

55   Alba Fucens: air view of site (Fot. 10576). See pp. 122–3.

56   Praeneste: air view of Fortuna temple site; early first century BC—upper part perhaps second century BC (Aerofototeca). See pp. 124–6.

57   Praeneste: model of Fortuna temple (Fot. 4348). See p. 126.

58   Tibur: so-called 'Temple of Vesta'; early first century BC (Fot. 10066). See p. 124.

59   Cora: Doric temple, *c*. 100 BC (Fot. 10454). See p. 124.

60   Pompeii: Temple of Apollo, first century BC (Fot. 2537). See p. 127.

61   Pompeii: Atrium of House of Surgeon, third century BC (F. Brown, *Rom. Architecture*). See p. 128.

62   Pompeii: air view of forum area and old part of city (Fot. 6446). See pp. 126–8.

63   Pompeii: garden peristyle of 'House of Vettii', second century BC (Fot. 2568). See p. 128.

64   Pompeii: painting from House of Lucretius Fronto, maritime 'villa' (Fot. 4939). See p. 129.

65   Herculaneum: 'Samnite House', atrium decorated in 'First Pompeian Style' (Alinari 43145). See pp. 128–9.

66   Avezzano: view of town and country; cast of relief found in Lake Fucino, mid-first century AD. (By courtesy of M. H. Bräude and Museo della civiltà romana.) See p. 129.

67 San Rocco: 'villa rustica', bedroom. See p. 131.

68 San Rocco: view of site. See pp. 130–1.

69 Posto: oil-separating vat. See p. 130.

70 Lucera: 'centuriation', with farms flanking road. *Cf.* J. Bradford, *Anc. Landscapes*, Ch. 4. See p. 132.

71 Lucera: farm. See p. 132.

72 Lucera: vine-trenches. See p. 132.

73 Lucera: farm site, with patio and oil tanks. See p. 132.

74, 'Caesarian' head, front and side. Cambridge: Fitzwilliam Mus. *Cf.* L.
75 Budde and R. Nicholls, *Catalogue of Greek and Roman Sculptures in Fitzwilliam Museum* (1964), no. 82 (p. 49). See p. 150.

76 Gladiatorial scene, late first century BC. Munich, Glyptothek (Ger. Arch. Inst. 5242). See p. 150.

77 Coins of Late Republic (denarii).
(a) Jupiter drawn by elephants, *C. METELLVS*. London: Brit. Mus. (Syd. 485, ? 113 BC). See pp. 140, 150.
(b) Sulla, *SVLLA. COS.* Brit. Mus. (Syd. 908; moneyer Q. Pompeius Rufus, *c.* 59 BC). See pp. 143–4.
(c) Coin of Fimbria in East (*c.* 85 BC): cistophoric tetradrachm, rev. with standard and caduceus (herald's staff), *FIMBRIA* and *IMPE.* Oxford: Ashmolean Mus. See p. 144.
(d) Venus, *L. BVCA.* Brit. Mus. (Syd. 1064, *c.* 44 BC). See p. 150.
(e, f) Libertas, *MAXSVMVS* (obv.); Roma and Venus, *C. EGNA-TIVS CN. F.* (rev.); Brit. Mus. (Syd. 787, *c.* 73 BC). See p. 150.
(g) Gaul: ? Vercingetorix. Brit. Mus. (Syd. 952; moneyer L. Hostilius Saserna, *c.* 48 BC). See p. 150.
(h) 'Gallia'. Brit. Mus. (Syd. 953; moneyer and date as for g). See p. 150.

78 Cato Uticensis from Volubilis, late first century BC, probably Augustan (Fot. 9176). See p. 162.

79 Cicero, late first century BC. Mus. Vat. (Alinari 6534). See p. 162.

80 Pompey, mid first century BC (Collection Frank E. Brown). *Cf. Studies presented to D. M. Robinson* (1951), p. 761 (pl. 95–97). See pp. 163–4.

81 Pompeian coins.
(a) (Aureus) Pompey in triumph. London: Brit. Mus. (Syd. 1028, ? 61 BC). See p. 164.
(b) (Denarius) Pompey, *CN. MAGNVS IMP.* Brit. Mus. (Syd. 1037a; moneyer M. Minatius Sabinus, 46–45 BC). See p. 164.
(c, d) (Aureus) Sextus Pompey, *MAG. PIVS. IMP. ITER.* (obv.); Pompey and his son Cnaeus, *PRAEF. CLAS. ET. OR. MARIT. EX S.C.* (rev.). Brit. Mus. (Syd. 1346a, 42–38 BC). See pp. 29, 164.

82 Coins illustrating Julius Caesar (denarii).
(a) Caesar, *CAESAR DICT. PERPETVO.* Cambridge, Fitzwilliam Mus. (*cf.* Syd. 1074; moneyer P. Sepullius Macer, *c.* 44 BC). See p. 169.
(b, c) Cap of liberty and daggers, *EID. MAR* (*Eidibus Martiis*; rev.); Brutus, left *L. PLAET. CEST.*, above and right *BRVT IMP* (obv.); Fitzwilliam Mus. (cf. Syd. 1301, 43–42 BC). See pp. 169–70.
(d) (Aureus): Octavia, *COS. DESIGN ITER. ET TER IIIVIR. R.P.C.* London: Brit. Mus. (Syd. 1200; coin of M. Antonius, 38–37 BC). See p. 171.

83 Head of Julius Caesar, mid first century BC, from Tusculum. See p. 167.

84 (a) Head of Antony, late first century BC. Narbonne, Musée archéologique municipal (Villani and Figli, Bologna). See p. 172.
(b) Tetradrachm. Antony, *ΑΝΤΩΝΙΟC [ΑΥΤΟΚΡΑΤΩΡ ΤΡΙ] ΤΟΝ ΤΡΙΩΝ ΑΝΔΡΩΝ* (rev.). Cambridge, Fitzwilliam Mus.

85 (a) Head of Cleopatra (nose restored), late first century BC. Mus. Vat. (Ger. Arch. Inst. 3986). See p. 172.

(b) Tetradrachm. Cleopatra, *BACIΛICCA ΚΛΕΟΠΑΤΡΑ [ΘΕΑ NE]ΩΤΕΡΑ* (obv.). Cambridge, Fitzwilliam Mus.

86 Octavian, Mus. Capit. (Anderson 1573). See pp. 171–2.

87 Coins of Octavian (Augustus).
(a) (Aureus) Augustus, *AVGVSTVS, c.* 20 BC. Cambridge, Fitz-william Mus.
(b, c) (Denarius) Crocodile, *AEGVPTO CAPTA* (rev.); Octavian, *CAESAR COS. VI* (obv.); 28 BC. Fitzwilliam Mus.

Index